W9-BIT-635

Vinny: Part II
THE STORY OF HABILITAT

Vinny: Part II

THE STORY OF HABILITAT

*by Vincent C. Marino
and Jerry Hopkins*

Edited by Jay Stewart

*VVM, Inc.
Kaneohe, Hawaii*

Published by VVM, Inc.
P.O. Box 801, Kaneohe, Hawaii 96744

Copyright 1987 by Vincent C. Marino and Jerry Hopkins.
All rights reserved.
Printed and bound in the United States of America.

ISBN 0-9610318-2-4 {pt. 2}

Library of Congress Cataloging in Publication Data
(Revised for part 2)

Marino, Vincent C. (Vincent Carmine), 1938–
  Vinny.

  Pt. 2 by Vincent C. Marino and Jerry Hopkins.
  Contents: [1] Victory over drugs, death, and
degradation—pt. 2. The story of Habilitat.
  1. Marino, Vincent C. (Vincent Carmine), 1938–
2. Narcotic addicts—United States—Biography.
3. Narcotic addicts—Rehabilitation—Hawaii—Case
studies. 4. Habilitat, inc. I. Stewart, Jay.
II. Hopkins, Jerry. III. Title.
HV5805.M367A38 1983   362.2'93'0924 [B]   82-24740
ISBN 0-9610318-0-8 (pt. 1)

ISBN 0-9610318-2-4 (pt. 2)

Design by Bee Webster Dietemann, Langfeld Associates
Production Coordination by Langfeld Associates
Typography by TBH/Typecast, Inc.
Printed and bound by the Maple-Vail Book Manufacturing Group.
Jackets printed by Lehigh Press.

TABLE OF CONTENTS

This book is dedicated to Gemma, my wonderful mother. You are gone but you will never be forgotten, and to my best friend Frank M. Cockett, Jr. "Boysan" who also helped me build Habilitat and was there whenever he was needed. I will never forget you.

ACKNOWLEDGEMENTS

To my beloved wife and partner, Vickie, who stood by me and helped me build Habilitat.

To my daughter, Victoria, who always gave me the inspiration I needed with her beautiful smile and understanding.

To Joe "Rocks," my wonderful father. I love you dearly.

To my secretary, Mary Ann O'Neill, without whose patience and perseverance this book would have taken as long to complete as did the Pyramids in Egypt.

Vinny: Part II

THE STORY OF HABILITAT

PREFACE

How will the 1980s in America be described to history students of the next century? Chances are that this incredibly chaotic period will be characterized as a time when the country anesthetized itself with an endless supply of mind-altering chemicals.

According to a National Institute on Drug Abuse survey, conducted in 1982, one-third of our household population (adults and children) has used an illicit drug. According to that same survey, there are currently over 20 million users of marijuana, 4.2 million users of cocaine, 1.6 million users of various types of sedatives, and 1.1 million users of tranquilizers. Moreover, though alcohol use is classified as legal, the fact of the matter is that over 100 million Americans are current users of that drug.

And if these statistics scare you, you should realize that they are based on information collected in 1982 and probably don't reflect the up-to-date figures accurately. Now usage rates are likely to be significantly higher. These figures also don't include all the legal prescription drugs millions misuse routinely.

The worst revelation of all is that drug addiction has spread from the ghettos and poverty areas of our inner cities to the affluent suburbs of middle America—to Main Street, U.S.A. This unchecked condition is unraveling the fabric of the American family.

It is not my intention in this book to preach about the evils of drug and alcohol addiction but rather to inform, educate, and maybe offer some hope to those personally afflicted with this pervasive condition. This book is also aimed at parents or others who are affected by the intrusion of drugs into their family unit. Even if a drug problem doesn't exist in your family right now, you can use the information in this book as a preventative reference work that you can reread from time to time to help you understand the ramifications of drug and alcohol abuse. It's a must for parents and parents-to-be.

It is a known fact that the recidivism rate for drug and alcohol abusers is extremely high. This means that the majority of users return to the use of illicit drugs and alcohol soon after their reentry into society, as reported by a range of treatment facilities. The drug and alcohol rehabilitation program at Habilitat, however, is the one facility that consistently reports the highest success rate in the country. Our unorthodox curriculum, which has been the brunt of much criticism, is paradoxically credited with a success rate of approximately 53 percent. The reason for this positive statistic in a sea of negatives is that Habilitat was hewn out of my own personal suffering and experience and tempered with the experience of others who have been able to pull themselves up by their boot-straps to rise out of the muck of drug and alcohol addiction.

Those of you who have read the book *Vinny: Victory Over Drugs, Death, and Degradation* have a good idea of what I have been through in my life. If you haven't, here's a synopsis.

I was born on December 22, 1938, on the lower east side of Manhattan in a section known as "Little Italy." My given name is Carmine Vincent Marino, but I've always answered to "Vinny." Times were hard then, after the tragic Depression and just before World War II.

I came from a relatively poor family, but we were rich in love for each other. I have two brothers—Frank, nineteen months older than me, and Joseph, eight years younger. My father, Joe "Rocks" Marino, was basically a decent human being, but he had a terrible gambling problem. He kept losing, and this got him into big trouble, causing him to be in and out of prison during most of my early years.

My mother, Gemma, was a strong and caring woman with deep religious convictions and high morals much like my father's mother, Rosa. My grandmother Rosa came to this country from Sicily at the age of fifteen. Widowed nine years later when my father was just a baby, she worked long hard hours as a seamstress to raise her four children. These two women always did their best to strengthen and improve our family life.

One of the disadvantages of being poor was that we were dependent on county hospitals, county doctors, and, of course, county-type treatment for our medical care, which brings me to my first bad memory. As a toddler of nineteen months, I was badly bitten on the lip by a vicious English bulldog. The injury left a scar I live with today, thanks to county hospital treatment, and it earned me the childhood nickname "Scarface." I didn't realize it then, but the mark left an even deeper emotional scar.

I was usually a pretty good kid, a little mischievous but not bad. I went to a parochial school, was an altar boy, and graduated grade school with honors. About that time, we left Little Italy and moved to a section in Brooklyn called "Borough Park." Home life was generally good, but I do have memories of bitter fights between my mother and father, usually instigated by my father's obsession with gambling and lost money.

When I reached fourteen, my world began to collapse. Perhaps because of my ugly facial scar, my self-esteem was very low. I felt inferior to my brothers, and it seemed to me that they received most of the attention and love at home so there wasn't much left for me. That was the situation when, one day— following another argument at home—I ran into a friend. On a dare—and seeking the acceptance of my peers—I took my first shot of heroin.

This is usually the way it happens, by the way: Low self-esteem coupled with peer pressure equals danger.

The euphoric feeling I experienced on the drug enabled me to block out my uncomfortable feelings of rejection and self-worthlessness. It was simple. I just made believe they didn't exist.

I took to heroin like an eagle takes to the sky, embarking on a fourteen-year roller coaster ride to hell. I was thrown out of five high schools by the time I was sixteen. My home life became an elaborate fabrication of lies and scams designed to cover up my heroin addiction and the various criminal activities I'd adopted to support it.

During those years, I amassed twenty-nine arrests, was given the last rites twenty-six times and, once—after a particularly bad drug overdose—I was pronounced dead. These events usually occurred in a hospital emergency room in one of the five boroughs of New York City. I was also kicked out of the army with an undesirable discharge and spent over five years in prison as a result of my nefarious escapades.

Somehow, in 1964, I made it into Synanon, a drug rehabilitation program in California, where I spent a year before I left. Then, in 1966, I entered Daytop Village, a drug rehabilitation program in Staten Island, New York. I stayed there for a year and then left. I learned something from each program but not enough to stop my life of drug addiction and crime.

In 1967, I went to Phoenix House in New York City where I stayed for a total of two and a half years. I was fighting for my life, and by then I was winning.

In these programs, I was a good student and tried to apply myself to the best of my abilities. After four and a half years in therapeutic communities, I discovered that maybe, just maybe, Vinny Marino really wasn't such a bad guy. I began to experience feelings of self-worth and self-confidence, which were reflected in the admiration and love my family and peers started to have for me. This was paramount in my developing a new feeling of self-love and self-respect.

Another thing that became obvious was my realization that I had a natural talent for working with others who had similar problems. I knew that this calling would be instrumental in surmounting the horrendous history I'd amassed. I also recognized that rather than trying to forget the fourteen years of my life that I had spent as a drug addict and criminal, I could put those awful memories to use as a tool to help others in similar situations. I vowed to dedicate my life to combating drug dependency.

At the end of my first book, I explained how I worked in several drug programs on the mainland and ended up in Hawaii, hired by a program called Communiversity. That job didn't work out, and I was preparing to return to the mainland when several residents of the program I was leaving

One of Habilitat's Sales Training Classes.

Residents can be trained in all fields of Carpentry.

approached me about staying. At their urging and with the encouragement of some Communiversity board members, I began to consider establishing a program of my own. That idea eventually became Habilitat.

In the book that follows, I tell about how Habilitat got its start and what it took to make Habilitat a reality. This is terribly important as it will give you an idea of the incredible odds I had to face to establish this concept. After all, the medical and clinical establishments meet any departure from the standard and accepted treatment procedures for drug abuse with resistance, but it is exactly that criticism which helped shape Habilitat into the most successful facility of its kind.

Part of what makes Habilitat so unusual is that the eighteen-month to two-year, live-in experience challenges the individual on every level without the use of traditional psychiatric approaches or psychotropic drugs of any kind. Instead, we teach self-reliance.

Encounter groups, one-on-one sessions, educational seminars, academic and vocational training all help direct the resident toward a lifestyle of positive values and high self-esteem—two of the things most lacking in a life dedicated to drugs or alcohol. Another factor is the importance we attach to education. Habilitat employs teachers from the Hawaii Department of Education at its on-site high school, and residents must obtain their diploma before finishing the program.

A significant highlight of our "survival school" is the extensive vocational-training opportunities. We believe that for a former drug addict to survive on the streets once he or she's been mainstreamed back into society that person must have a viable trade or skill. Otherwise, it's almost certainly back to a life of drugs and booze. For this reason, we operate many small businesses, including landscaping, construction, painting, masonry, housecleaning, food service, baking, sales,

Volleyball game in the courtyard.

Vinnie leading a seminar on Habilitat's concepts.

and telemarketing. We also put on a number of special events each year, including a rodeo, a new product show, and a family exposition. Training in these real business activities provides each resident with the opportunity to develop good work habits and immense pride along with at least one brand-new skill.

These businesses also contribute greatly to another unique aspect of Habilitat. We are the only long-term residential program I know of that is entirely self-supporting. Unlike others, we do not take government funding. We used to, but we quickly learned that with every ten dollars worth of help, you get a guy with a rule book and a clipboard telling you how to spend it.

I believe that anyone with imagination and dedication can duplicate what Habilitat has done, and I sincerely hope that programs like Habilitat will be started in other communities. It is my fondest wish that this book inspire people in other cities to try creating their own successful rehabilitation programs.

I believe that the future of the world lies with our children and that those children are now threatened as they've never been before. There is no place in a sane world for the kind of substance abuse that is raging throughout our country today. We must do something. We must *all* do something. To this end, I have dedicated my life.

Vinny Marino
Honolulu, 1986

Chapter One

SO THIS IS PARADISE

Coming to Hawaii did not seem to be the brightest thing I'd ever done. I began swearing at myself and the rest of the world while I yanked open bureau drawers and emptied their contents into my suitcase. Pam, the woman I had met after only a few days in Hawaii, moved to the closet and began to pull my shirts and trousers out. As she folded the clothes and laid them on the bed, she said, "Take it easy, Vinny."

I yelled back at her, "How can I take it easy? I had my heart set on making this job work for me. I failed at Synanon, I failed at Daytop Village, and I failed at Phoenix House. I failed at the Columbia University Medical Center in New York City, and I failed at RAP. Now I end up in Hawaii, failing at Communiversity, six thousand miles from home. You know, Pam, I learned a lot about people over the past five years—especially people like me. I learned what it takes to help them turn their lives around. All my contacts are on the mainland. I wouldn't even know where to start here."

Pam came over and stood in front of me, her sweet face solemn. She looked into my eyes and spoke quietly, 'Calm down, Vinny. You found this job, and you'll find another one in Hawaii. You've made some good friends, and I'll help you any way I can. Now, let's finish up and get out of here."

She returned to packing while I slumped into a chair by the desk and watched her work. After a minute or so, I said, "Pam?"

She raised her head and looked at me.

I said, "Thanks for the pep talk. I'm sorry I yelled at you, and I realize how lucky I am to have you, even if it doesn't always look that way. Maybe it's not a question that I really failed at those programs. They just weren't ready for my ideas and didn't let me implement what I felt would work." She smiled and went back to her work, and I began to sort my papers and books into boxes. As I worked, I went over everything that had happened.

Less than two months before, I had been working at the Regional Addiction Program (RAP) in Washington, D.C., when I acccidentally intercepted a telephone call from Hawaii. I recognized the name, Rizocatta. I thought it was an old acquaintance of mine whose first name was Tony, but it was his exwife, whose name was Ima. She had called to check on the references of someone she employed who she thought was using drugs. Ima also told me that she had started a drug rehabilitation program called Communiversity and that she was looking for a person who could handle the job of director of induction.

At the time she called, winter was closing in on Washington, D.C., and as she talked, I started fantasizing about bare-breasted women, swaying palm trees, and thatched huts on the shores of paradise. She asked if I was interested in the job, and it didn't take me long to accept her offer.

At the time, a lot of people thought I was insane to accept because Hawaii had been a state for only eleven years. My brother, Frank, took me to the airport, but while he was hugging me and saying goodbye, he asked me, "Brother, do you know what you're doing? You're going to be six thousand miles away."

I looked at him as I kissed and hugged him and said, "Frank, I'm not sure, and I realize that it's a long way from where I was raised. But let me tell you this, I want to make my mark and Hawaii's as good a place as any!"

Late that night, when I arrived in Hawaii, Ima and one of her key staff members welcomed me with a kiss and a fragrant lei of bright flowers. We drove to the facility, which was on the leeward side of the island, some distance away. I was completely wiped out after the eleven-hour nonstop flight from New York and as soon as she showed me to my room, I undressed, climbed into bed, and fell asleep.

The next morning, I got up early. After breakfast, Ima showed me around the facility and introduced me to the residents. She also explained the responsibilities of my new position, which involved bringing residents into the program. I was extremely enthusiastic about the program because it was relatively new. She had only thirteen residents, and I wanted to prove to myself I had whatever goods it would take to be successful.

Within a few weeks, I brought in a couple of dozen new people, and the place was buzzing with activity. There wasn't much time to relax under the swaying palms or socialize with the hula girls I had fantasized about back in Washington, D.C., but I liked most of what I had seen of Hawaii. The weather was great, and the facility was located in an old sugar plantation hospital in a country village called Ewa. Sugar cane grew all around the buildings we occupied, and there were plenty of palm trees, which gave the place a tropical feeling.

I also found a new girlfriend, Pam, so I felt pretty good as I drove into Honolulu to learn my way around the Hawaiian court system, to the hospitals and prisons, and to Waikiki, where most of the drugs seemed to be.

When it came to drugs, there was definitely trouble in paradise. Waikiki may have had the world's most famous beach —then at its absolute peak season in December and January— but it also had a busy drug clinic. The headlines in the local papers during that period made the drug problem clear. In January 1971 alone news stories said, "Drug flow to isles increases. . ." "Camp Smith marines want drug education forums," "'Stoned' at Waianae; student drug use aired . . ." "Drugs are major problem in Oahu schools." It seemed like a challenge to me so I made up my mind to stay and go for broke.

Then, unexpectedly, about seven weeks after arriving in Hawaii, I found myself caught up in a bitter hassle with Ima. She accused me of not following orders and trying to usurp her authority, which I completely denied.

Considering the short time I had been there, I was happy I had the support of the residents as well as the backing of the Communiversity board of directors. But I was determined to avoid a confrontation with Ima because I did not want to get the residents involved. She solved that problem for me, however.

On January 27, she called a special board meeting and included the staff, which meant me too. We were all seated when Ima entered the room and handed a sheaf of papers to each one of us. The packet turned out to be a new set of bylaws firing me and the entire board of directors.

The board members seemed stunned. In the confusion, Dr. Neil Winn, the chairman, tried to restore calm and clarify the situation. Suddenly I had had enough of Ima's power plays and her insanity. I rose to my feet and told Ima she was completely out of order and did not know what she was doing. I then said my goodbyes and left the room.

On the way to my cottage her boyfriend Steve tried to stop me from going in to pick up my belongings. He stood in front of me. I said, "Look, Steve, I know you don't want a beef with me, and I don't want a beef with you. But I promise you, if you don't get out of my way and let me get my things, I'll leave you on the floor for dead."

He stepped aside. Pam came running up, and together we walked back to my room in the staff house. I tried to explain what had happened, and thirty minutes later, we were finished with my packing. Pam took a last look around the room while I snapped my suitcase shut.

Just then we heard a commotion in the hall, and someone was pounding on the door. Pam opened the door to find a young female resident named Maria, who was sobbing hysterically and demanding to see me. Pam explained that we were leaving, but Maria was insistent—she had to see me.

Finally Pam brought her into the room and persuaded her to sit down. Through her sobs she kept pleading to be allowed to leave with me. Within a few minutes, five other residents joined us, all determined not to be left behind. Since I had brought all of them into Communiversity by promising them it was a good program, I felt an obligation toward them. I pointed out that it was already late in the evening, and I had no idea where I was going. They countered my logic with threats that they would return to the streets, use drugs, or act insanely if I refused to take them along. At last I agreed, wondering how in the hell I was going to find a place to put all of us up for night. More important, I wondered, what were we going to do tomorrow.?

As we were leaving the building, a young married couple named Bob and Rosie, graduates of the Mendocino Family Drug Program in California and also on Ima's staff, approached me. They said that they were fed up with Ima and asked if they could come along with me too.

At first I was hesitant because neither of them had ever backed me in any of my disputes with Ima over the way she was handling the kids and the entire facility. But then I figured, two more couldn't make that much difference, and they might be helpful in handling the others. I was beginning to feel like the Pied Piper of Honolulu.

We all agreed our most immediate need was to find housing for the night. With no place to go and little money in my pocket, it was a big problem. We decided our best bet would be to head into town to the Waikiki Drug Clinic and call some of the board members who had been fired that evening. Maybe they could help us.

The ten of us piled into Pam's car, Bob and Rosie's car, and mine and left Communiversity. To say that I was scared out of my skin would not accurately describe my feelings. Here I was, not forty days in Hawaii, without a job after breaking my back daily, running around town inducting people and bringing them into the program. I thought I had finally found a place where I could hang my hat, live in peace, and do the thing that I loved doing most—turning people around so that they could lead productive, happy lives without the crutch of chemicals. And look what happened.

As we were driving, a rush of thoughts and feelings went through me. Was it Ima's fault or was I right? I was in one hell of a spot, stuck with six residents, a brand-new girlfriend, and two staff members that one, I really didn't trust, and two, I resented. Maybe the controversy with Ima could have been resolved in a more amicable fashion if they had spoken up. One thing was sure—my mind was working overtime.

Within a couple of hours we were meeting with two of the board members—Neal Winn and a man named Mickey Hummer, who worked with the legal-aid department. Both were men of intelligence, spirit, and integrity, and they carried a lot of weight in their community. I highly respected them, and their trust and encouragement meant much to me.

We hashed over the evening's events, and I think it was then I began to wonder if I could come up with a workable solution of my own. The first order of business, though, was to find a place to sleep. Neal suggested that we get hotel rooms—one for the girls and one for the guys, one for Bob and Rosie, and one for me. I vetoed the idea quickly.

"Neal," I said, "with all due respect, I can visualize the horrified reaction of any Waikiki hotel manager we ask to turn over four rooms, without reservations, to nine different people. Besides that, I'd like to keep these kids all together, not only for moral support, but because I don't want them in Waikiki. That's where most of them got into trouble in the first place."

About then Mickey said, "Vinny, I own a small house in Kailua. It's empty right now, and it would be a place to stay for a few days until we can sort out the situation at Communiversity."

The kids were enthusiastic, and I jumped at the chance. "That's great, Mickey, just tell us how to get there. I'd like to get everyone settled for the night."

He volunteered to show us the way, and Neal wanted to be sure that everything went smoothly, too, so he decided to come along. Now our caravan had five cars, as the twelve of us headed up into the mountains in a torrential, tropical rainstorm. Raindrops the size of silver dollars fell on us in silver sheets as we inched up the steep slopes. I wasn't familiar with this part of the island so Mickey led the way, and I followed.

I swore repeatedly and a couple of the girls giggled nervously as I eased the car around hairpin curves and down the steep windward side of the mountain. Just when I had about decided I had missed the turn and driven into the ocean, we reached level ground, and the rain let up. We found Mickey pulled over the side of the road waiting for us. He leaned out his car window to wave at us. "How do you like Hawaii now, Vinny?"

We followed Mickey through the quiet streets of the little town into an attractive residential neighborhood where he pulled up in front of a small house. A light rain was still falling, and it dripped from tall trees onto the neat green lawn.

Mickey opened the door to the house and turned on the lights. One of them lit up the swimming pool in the backyard, and even in the rain it looked beautiful. As we all followed Mickey into the house, he kept repeating that although the house was small it would handle our needs, at least for the night. It may have looked small to him, but to us, it looked wonderful. There were two and a half bedrooms, a bath and a half, a kitchen, and a fair-sized living room. Except for a pool table, one couch, and a small chair, the house had no furniture, but I figured most of us were tired enough to sleep standing up.

I took Pam's hands and led her into the kitchen. She looked so tired. I put my arms around her and pulled her close. I wished we had a place to be alone, but already several faces were peeking around the edge of the door. I started to jokingly yell at them, but Pam broke in with a laugh as she moved out of my arms. After she told the others good night, I walked out to her car and kissed her.

"You are one fantastic lady," I said, as she pulled away. She waved, and I stood in the driveway until I could no longer see her car.

I turned back to the house, breathing deeply of the cool, clean night air. Through the lighted windows, I watched the kids moving from room to room when, suddenly, I felt overwhelmed with the enormity of the job I had taken on. For a minute I felt like turning my back and walking away into the night, but my conscience began to argue back right away. Okay, Vinny, it said, here's your big chance. You've been telling people all across the country what's wrong with their rehab programs. Now you can show them how you think it ought to be done.

Chapter Two

GROWING, GROWING, GROAN

I was awakened in the morning by the excited animated voices of the kids. The rain had stopped, and the sun was bright and hot. Since I hadn't gotten to sleep until about 4:30 A.M., I figured the day would be just as beautiful if it started a few hours later, and I'd be in better shape to appreciate it.

"How in the hell can they be so cheerful so early?" I muttered. I closed my eyes and tried to go back to sleep, but every joint and muscle in my body ached from hours of tossing on the hard floor.

I struggled to my feet, stretched my tormented muscles, and buttoned myself into the shirt I'd been using for a pillow. Through the open window I could see the kids laughing and playing around the swimming pool. I glared at them and stomped into the bathroom, where I shaved and showered quickly, annoyed that I had only the one small towel I had borrowed from Ima's house.

Then I started to laugh. How could I get upset over a small towel? I had no sheets and no beds to put them on if I had them. I had no chairs, no tables — except for the pool table (which would prove useful as a bed later) — no sofas, no rugs, no dishes. I had no food to put on the dishes I didn't have either. And the small amount of money I had wouldn't last long with all the demands I was about to put on it.

I joined the kids in the yard. That was one thing I did have — plenty of kids and all of them needing things I didn't have. Nobody was complaining though, and that made me feel good. I told them that I was going out to get breakfast. I jumped into my car and went out to buy coffee and donuts. By the time I got back to the house Mickey was already there with a couple of sleeping bags and some blankets he had rounded up. We thanked him and he left, promising to be back with more supplies soon. We tidied the place up, and then I gathered everyone around me for a meeting. We talked about our situation and what we could do.

I could see the kids were apprehensive and anxious, and I explained that I honestly had no idea what I was going to do and that I didn't see how it would be possible for us to stay in the house much longer. They became a bit upset. As a matter of fact a couple of the girls were crying. But I felt I had to be honest with them, and at that point I could see no future for our group.

About that time, Mickey returned and then in walked Neal. Both brought bedding, linens, and enough food to get us through a day or two. They showed the girls where the washer and dryer were. A little later Pam showed up with dishes, glasses, silverware, and a couple of brooms and mops. She even brought pots and pans, a coffee pot, some bread and peanut butter. Then she stayed and helped us put together a pile of peanut butter sandwiches, and we all ate lunch together.

The kids were relaxed and content again, hoping everything was okay. But I was looking further down the road than tonight's dinner, and I knew our problems were not over. If anything, they were getting worse because that afternoon four more kids left Communiversity to join us. I didn't know how they got the word so fast, but they did and within a week our population grew from six to sixteen. The only feeling that I really could relate to when that sixteenth person walked through the door was stark fear.

I began to start talking to myself: Vinny, what the hell are you doing? You're in Hawaii, how far can you go with this thing? There's very little money, a small house. What if a bunch more people wanted to come in? How are you going to house them? How are you going to feed them? And how far are you going to go with it? The feeling I had was as big a fear as I used to have when I was out on the streets, scamming people, never knowing when I would catch a bullet in the back or wind up doing some heavy time.

And I thought about the troops. What about Maria? She was the one who had gotten hysterical and convinced me to take her with me when I left Communiversity. She was only sixteen, and although she had a home to go back to, she didn't want to go. Her parents were divorced, and she was convinced she was unloved. She didn't have any drug problems, but her other problems were real enough.

What about Alice and her brother Todd? They were fifteen and eighteen. Again it was a family thing, and he was into pot. He was also about to be drafted, and he told me that he'd run away to Canada if he didn't have us.

What about Beverly, a local girl, seventeen years old, who

every time we gave her a "haircut" (firm, constructive criticism) cried big crocodile tears and silently began foaming at the mouth?

What about Kimo? He was the wildest of them all, the one who had the most trouble suppressing his urge for violence. I don't think there was a drug he hadn't used, and his personality had suffered—the more he used, the nastier he got, until nasty is all he thought he was.

One by one, I ticked off their names, shaking my head. As soon as I could, I got together with Neal and Mickey and explained that I couldn't be responsible for these people. I said I felt an obligation to the kids since I had talked them into entering Communiversity, and I would try to stay in Hawaii until either they returned to their homes if that was possible, or I could find a safe place for them to live. I made it clear that I planned to return to the mainland as soon as this was accomplished.

I saw fear in Neal's and Mickey's eyes, and they immediately tried to convince me that they could get the money problem straightened out and things would work out. They wanted to establish a program based in Kailua, to be called Windward Communiversity, and suggested that Bob and I could function as codirectors. They asked me to please be patient for at least a few days while they arranged for me to meet with the rest of the board of directors from Communiversity. Relunctantly, I agreed.

At the meeting I was advised that the board was bringing suit against Ima since she had supposedly withdrawn $50,000 of Communiversity's funds and put it into a cashier's check that she refused to return. At that time she claimed she was the founder of Communiversity, a defenseless woman, and a bunch of volunteer, professional people were trying to take her program away from her. I imagine the $50,000 represented some sort of security so that she could at least last long enough to go through the upcoming lawsuit.

The board hired a flamboyant attorney named David Schutter, and he and I had an instant rapport. Unfortunately, ours was the first case David ever lost. He proved, however, to be a valuable friend and ally of Habilitat.

He called about a week later to tell me about one of his clients, Frank Cockett. Frank was a Maui boy, young, married, with a kid. He was into barbiturates and alcohol, and when his wife threatened to leave him and take their son, he got a shotgun and threatened to kill her and her mother and father and to take the child.

The way it ended, Frank drove his car into a tree and broke his jaw among other injuries. He was treated at a local hospital, arrested, and formally charged with attempted murder, attempted kidnapping, and possession of a firearm. He was then sent to the state hospital on the island of Oahu.

After I hung up the phone with Dave I made arrangements with Frank's family to have him brought to me, with the understanding that if I did not, for whatever reasons, accept him into the program, my advice would be for them to have him sent back to the hospital so that he couldn't get into further trouble.

When Frank came over, we paired him up with four local guys—two from the island of Maui, the other two from Oahu—to take him on a tour of our facility while I sat down to talk with his parents.

After our conversation had gone on for about half an hour, with some rather probing questions from me, I knew that Frank was a lazy, selfish, self-centered individual who didn't care about anybody in the world, had no knowledge of the word *respect*, wanted what he wanted when he wanted it, and became abusive not only to his parents but also to his wife and her family when he didn't get what he wanted. And things got worse as he became more and more involved with drugs and alcohol.

I ended the conversation, sent for Frank, and asked the same young residents to escort Mr. and Mrs. Cockett around the facility so they could feel more comfortable about where and with whom he would be living and see what the program entailed. As I asked Frank to have a seat, it was easy for me to tell that I was face to face with an arrogant, cocky, young punk.

I told Frank I had only two reasons for bothering with him. First, having met his parents, I felt a lot of empathy for them. They reminded me of my parents, who had put up with a lot of shit from me. Second, Dave Schutter was a good friend, and he had asked if we could be of some help because Frank had a serious drug problem and Dave didn't want to see him go to prison where he would receive no help.

A lot of people still think jails rehabilitate. These are the same people who have no idea that 1 out of every 450 Americans is in jail. (Only the Soviet Union and South Africa have a higher percentage of their citizens locked up.) How many of them, do you think, are improved by the experience? The truth is that all jails do today is punish and warehouse.

I believed my program could become a real, workable alternative to prison, one that placed 100 percent of its effort into what the jails gave up on—the reconstruction of the individual. Whenever I hear somebody call a jail a "correctional facility," I have to laugh—or cry.

I told Frank he really had no choice. Either he entered the program or he would go to prison. Emphatically I painted an ugly picture. I also explained that I could not guarantee I could get him probated to us from both Maui and the federal court here on our island. However, I emphasized that if this were possible, he would have to remain with us until he was clinically discharged. Otherwise he would be in violation of the court's stipulation.

I also explained that although Dave Schutter and his parents got him as far as my office, it would be impossible for him to become a resident unless he passed a rigid interview conducted by me and some of his peers. Unless he could convince us that he was willing to abide by our rules and do things our way, then the same door he entered was the way he could leave and sort out his own problems.

He shrugged and said, "Well, I guess I have no choice. Let's go with the interview."

I said, "Look, asshole, I don't know where you think you are or who the hell you think you're talking to, but what I'm going to tell you in all honesty is that I don't like your attitude, and we definitely don't need you. You seem like you've got all the ingredients to become one royal pain in the ass. I'm not your mother and I'm not your father so I'm not going to put up with your bullshit, and I want that clear right here and now. If you don't like that and your attitude doesn't change immediately, you might as well get the hell out of here now. We're not running Sunnybrook Farm."

I could see the change in Frank's face immediately, and what bit of humility he could muster showed. I sent for the residents and instructed them to put Frank in the prospect chair. I then spoke briefly and said good-bye to Mr. and Mrs. Cockett and told them we would be in touch but to have some faith because it looked like we had enough leverage to turn him around.

For the next five hours, Frank sat waiting for the interview to begin. Keeping a person waiting was a technique I found to be invaluable. It gives the potential resident a chance to observe what is going on. He is totally ignored by everyone, but he can't help noticing that everyone is working, contributing something to the environment.

All around Frank, Maria, Kimo, and the others went about their daily chores — cleaning the bathrooms and woodwork and floors, checking in food as it arrived, then making everyone lunch, picking up leaves on the lawn, and sweeping the area around the pool. They washed windows. They washed clothes. They even washed my car. The idea was to let Frank know that this program was not some halfway house where a person can sit and watch TV all day.

As he was watching us, we were watching him, too. You can learn a lot about someone who has to sit and wait for an unreasonable amount of time. It's a small pressure, but it's pressure nonetheless, and Frank reacted predictably.

He was getting nervous as he sat. At first he was puzzled, and then, after several hours, he got bored and impatient. He was not permitted to daydream and go to sleep, however. He was told to stay alert but to keep quiet. He was not allowed to talk either.

When he was finally called into my office, two residents from Maui, two other male residents, and I immediately started bombarding him. First, we attacked his attitude and how he had walked on the property thinking he was hot stuff. Second, we stressed that we didn't feel he actually realized the amount of trouble he was in because he figured David Schutter would get him out.

One of the Maui guys said, "You're really funny, Frank. You walk around like you're a tough guy, and because your jaw is wired up, you're going to have to be eating out of a straw for the next three or four months. You know what, sucker, if we decide not to accept you, you'll be running that Bruce Lee act in the state or the federal penitentiary, whichever one they send you to. You better knock it off and understand that this isn't Maui, and we're not the guys you were raised with. We're also here because if not, we'd be in jail. Now, let's get down to the nitty-gritty—what do you want from us?"

Frank didn't know how to act. He looked at me and said, "What is it *you* want?"

"Hey Frank, I don't want anything. The only thing I really want to tell you is that so far we've wasted a lot of time playing this fucking game of yours. The one that's in trouble is you, not us."

In the ensuing conversation, we learned how long he had been using drugs and what type, how long he had been drinking and to what extent. We also learned that he really didn't want to work and was very lazy and was also flippant and sarcastic—altogether a swaggering Mr. Macho Man.

Another thing he told us: His nickname on Maui was "Oiler"—meaning someone who was slimy, slippery, and couldn't be trusted. We all started to ridicule him and make fun of the name *Oiler,* and I told him the kind of involvement he'd experienced on the streets was going to be totally different here. At that point Frank started to get a little more serious, and he asked again what we wanted from him?

I look at him dead in the eyes, and said, "Well, to begin with we're going to shave your head, but first you have to ask for our help."

He wanted to know why we were going to shave his head, and he was simply told "That's the way it is. We don't give reasons around here and, frankly, it's none of your goddamned business. You don't have a choice except to leave."

He then asked for help.

One of the residents, a kid named Philly, said, "Louder."
Frank yelled louder.

Then another kid, Bobby, said, "Louder, I can't hear you."
It was very difficult for me to keep a straight face because

it's hard enough to scream under those circumstances, much less with his physical impairment.

When we thought he had enough I said, "Frank, what is it you really want?"

With tears running from his eyes, he said, "I want some help. I don't want to go to prison. I'm sorry for what I did. I'm sorry I came over here acting like a wise guy. I'm not really a wise guy. I just felt that my wife was trying to steal my kid from me. I'm willing to do whatever you tell me, but please keep me out of prison."

Again I looked at him straight and said, "Okay, we'll accept you." With that, we all got up, and I started first to hug him and say, "Welcome." Then all the residents did the same.

Finally the day came to go to court. Frank was facing a federal charge in Honolulu and a state charge on Maui. The first court appearance was on Maui, and I have to admit I lied in court. I told the judge I'd already talked to the federal judge on Oahu and said he'd promised to give Frank a break.

The judge on Maui said, "Well, if the judge in Honolulu is giving him a break, I will, too."

I then came back to Oahu and told the judge here that the judge on Maui was giving Frank probation if he went along. And he did. It worked!

The next case was not so successful. A woman called me up about her daughter Linda who was sixteen years old. She asked for an appointment, and when she came, I had four females show Linda around the property and explain the program while I spoke to her mother. The mother was very nervous and was stuttering constantly during our conversation.

It turned out that Linda was using drugs, the mother didn't really know what kind, and also drinking rather heavily. She had taken Linda to a few psychiatrists and psychologists but to no avail. She didn't know where to go or who to turn to, and someone at a local social service agency referred her to us.

She explained that one afternoon when she came home unexpectedly, Linda was on the bed, nude, with three young men, also nude. She screamed at them to get dressed and chased them out of the house and then tried to take control of Linda, who at that point was rather incoherent. She made a quick pot of coffee, helped Linda into the bathtub, and gave her first a warm and then a cool bath, followed by a cooler shower to wake her up.

Then she asked, "What's going on? Who are these people? Why are you in this kind of shape?"

Linda's response was semicoherent: "What people? What shape? I'm okay Mom, I must have just had a little too much to drink."

From that time until the meeting with me she wouldn't let Linda out of her sight, which meant that she didn't go to work, and if she had to go to the store, she took Linda with her. She told me that if this was what she had *seen* happen, imagine what was going on that she didn't see because many nights Linda had come home real late, looking disheveled, and obviously intoxicated.

"For all I know, it could have been drugs or a combination of both."

I told her I'd heard enough and had the girls bring Linda to my office and show the mother around the facility.

When I spoke to Linda, she seemed very high strung, couldn't look me straight in the eye, and was real fidgety. I explained what her mother had told me. She candidly said that although she didn't realize what had really happened that night, that was not the first time this type of situation had occurred. I asked Linda if this made her happy?

She replied, "No."

I then asked her what kind of drugs she was using.

"I use all kinds, but mainly barbiturates, and I drink a lot, mostly vodka."

I said that it might be in her interest to enter our program and try to find out why these deliberate attempts to kill herself were taking place. I explained that we had a long-range program and that the drugs and/or alcohol were not really the problem but only the symptoms, like a fever, a sign that something was wrong organically. The same applied to whatever drugs and alcohol she was consuming—they were not her problem, but just a symptom of how she felt about herself. Linda seemed interested and agreed to come into the program.

I sent for her mother and explained that it was best to say a quick good-bye, that our procedure was to cut off all family ties for approximately two or three months, but that we would have Linda write her a letter within a week to let her know how she finds the program. Then if she wants to, she can call once or twice a month to find out what Linda's progress is, and after Linda earns the right to have a visit, that would be arranged.

Everything seemed to be going along fine until Linda started crying hysterically. She begged her mom, "Please take me home. I don't want to stay here. I don't want to have to be anyplace for two years. I promise I'll be good, I won't use drugs anymore, I'll go back to school, I won't fool around with guys. I swear to you Mom, I've learned my lesson. Please give me one last chance."

With that, her mother started crying. "Linda, I'm afraid that maybe next time I might not be around to help you."

But being as manipulative as most drug addicts are, male or female, Linda convinced her mother along with making her feel guilty by saying, "After all, I'm your daughter. How can you leave me in a place like this and just turn your back on me, when in fact I really think you should help me. Probably if you and Dad had gotten along I would have been much more happy, and I would never have gotten into drugs. But I swear to you, I've learned my lesson. Please take me home, please give me one more chance."

Linda's mom looked at me and said, "Vinny, I can't leave her. She obviously doesn't want to stay, and I really want to believe that she's learned her lesson and is going to do the right thing."

I looked at her and said, "Whatever you want to do is up to you. What we've got here is strictly self-help. I can only tell you that Linda needs a highly controlled, structured environment. Otherwise there is a strong possibility she might get into serious trouble. On the other hand, if you're going to let her manipulate you as she's done in the past, and you want to go along with it, then I can't be of any help. I strongly recommend that you get her into some place where she can be under strict supervision, and I wouldn't waste a lot of time doing it."

She thanked me and asked me to convey my thanks to the female residents who had showed her around. I walked her to the door and said, "Please remember what I told you. It's important for Linda's welfare."

Three days later Linda was found dead from an overdose of a combination of barbiturates and alcohol on a bench in Kapiolani Park in Honolulu.

Chapter Three

MOMENT OF TRUTH: MIND

In the next few weeks, as the population in the house grew to twenty-two, I continued to meet with members of the Communiversity board. While I kept insisting to myself and to them that I was still returning to the mainland, at the same time I was running all over town—to family court, circuit court, Halawa Jail, the state hospital, and the kids' detention home, actively recruiting more people, which made no sense at all. I also accepted all those who found us on their own or by word of mouth.

Actually, as I think back, I can't imagine how I functioned with two such contradictory goals. Maybe I was still playing out the role of the director of induction, or perhaps I had already decided to stay but hadn't admitted it to myself. Probably it was a combination of both. At any rate, during the day, Bob and

Rosie held the fort at the facility while I kept busy promoting and pitching the program. Although I wanted no part of the name *Communiversity*, it was all I had to identify our facility. Besides, that was what the board of directors wanted the facility to be called.

We were getting fantastic support from the Windward Coalition of Ministers. The only problem was that in order to get the food and supplies the organization furnished so generously, we also had to accept a lot of fellowship and well-meant proselytizing, which turned most of our kids off. I laid down some pretty stiff rules for this situation. I explained to each kid that if they couldn't handle the situation, they should come to me, and I would get them off the hook. I'm sure at times that some of our benefactors must have been shocked at the language they heard, especially from the newcomers. However, they hung in with us, and we made some good friends.

We were getting it together by now. We had printed signs designating certain areas as "Director's Office," "Kitchen," "Recreation Area," and so on. The place was spotless, we were eating fairly regularly, and we were making ourselves known and liked in the neighborhood. We had helped our neighbors with their yard work and had cleaned the streets and sidewalks, and we did our best to be an asset to the area. In the early mornings we jogged through the streets singing, and soon nearly everyone in Kailua knew who we were.

After everything was cleaned at the house, the troops sometimes started in all over again. To some it might have looked like busywork, but it wasn't. The idea was to keep everyone occupied so they couldn't dwell on their desire for alcohol or drugs or being somewhere else.

In between jobs were encounter groups and talks from me on some of the ideas I wanted them to learn. A lot of it came from what I myself had learned at Synanon, Daytop

Village, and Phoenix House. For example, I said that if you act *as if* long enough, soon enough you become. That was from Emerson. From Thomas Edison I took another lesson: *If the mind of man can conceive and believe, he can achieve.* Jean-Paul Sartre was an existentialist, but he was right on when he said that *life was never fair.* Another of my favorites was Saul Alinsky, who believed the little guy could win but only if he helped himself.

I told them the four cardinal rules: no alcohol or drugs, no violence or threat of violence, no sex, no stealing.

When I was in other rehabilitation programs, I developed some of my own sayings—things that made a person think a little. Like:

"Yesterday, today was tomorrow. What happened? Tomorrow, today will be yesterday. What did you accomplish?"

I'd ask the troops what that meant to them. It started them thinking about goals.

From the beginning, I encouraged everyone to read. Some of these kids had never read even a newspaper, and I insisted they learn to do that. I used *Six Weeks to Words of Power* by Wilfred Funk to encourage them to increase their vocabulary and use unfamiliar words. We set up a blackboard in a highly visible area, and every day we learned one new word. We called it "the word of the day" and everyone had to learn its meaning and how to spell it and had to use it at least ten times.

The response to my efforts was amazing. It's probably true that our general population didn't include many who would become nuclear physicists or astronauts, but their positive reaction to a little mental stimulation was deeply gratifying. Many had never been exposed to much education before, and those who had been exposed had rejected it. I don't know why they were receptive now, but I believe the fact that they trusted and believed in me had a great deal to do with it. They knew I was for real and that I'd once walked in their shoes.

I also established a policy regarding the residents' personal belongings, which insured that no problems would arise because one person had more material possessions than another. These rules still apply today. When residents come into the program, they are told what they should bring with them: sneakers, socks, work clothes, underwear, handkerchiefs, and a couple of pairs of dress clothes: Nothing formal or overly dressy, maybe four or five work outfits—dungarees, sports shirts, or blouses. If the new resident arrives with more than this, he or she is given the option of sending it home or donating it to the program.

The same rule applies to cash or personal property such as radios, electric razors, and so on. Later, when residents have been here for a while and are doing well in the program, they are allowed to write or phone home and request some personal belongings. In this way, they learn that they must earn all privileges. They also learn that there is no free lunch in life, and you get nothing for nothing—anything you get definitely must be earned.

During that period we did have one unfortunate neighborhood experience. We lived next door to a family with several teenage kids. Their parents left for a long trip, and the kids threw a series of parties that lasted until morning and included booze and drugs. On a day following one of these parties we found an almost empty bottle of vodka near the hedge on our side of the backyard. Of course we allowed no alcohol on our property. I immediately questioned our people about it, and they all denied any knowledge of it. I guessed what had happened, but I had no proof. I figured that these guys next door probably resented us so much that they deliberately put that bottle on our side of the fence to undermine our program.

We waited, and the same thing happened the next time they had a party. And on the third occasion, we actually saw the kids push a bottle through the hedge into our yard. Aside from that, we were constantly rained with small stones thrown from their side of the fence over to ours. I became furious. I gathered several of my biggest, toughest, ugliest guys, and we paid a visit next door. I told the kids I knew what had happened and demanded an apology. One of them got abusive with me, and in the heat of the moment I informed him I intended to remove part of his face. Of course we didn't actually touch anybody, but these people were trying to set us up, and I was really angry.

When we returned to our house, some of my guys decided we needed to sit down and talk about what had happened. One said, "Hey Vince, you've taught us that one of your cardinal rules is no violence or threat of violence. Yet you violated that tenet and at the same time you're asking us to trust your judgment. What's going on?"

I felt embarrassed and ashamed because they were absolutely right. I told them the truth. I said, "Okay, I blew it. I was wrong and I apologize but I'm only human. However, if we had not caught these people, one or two of you guys might eventually have gotten blamed and thrown out. You might have wound up back in prison or in the streets shooting dope, possibly dying. I guess I just lost my head, but it's because I care. I can promise you this, however, it will never happen again!"

The next day, our neighbors wrote a letter to the local newspaper saying that for no reason, they had been threatened by us, specifically me. Sensing a lurid story, the newspaper prepared to play it up big. Fortunately, a friend of mine on the newspaper staff intercepted the letter and called me. I immediately went down and met with the editor. I explained our version, the entire truth. In the meantime, the parents

next door had returned home, and I also told them what happened. The story never appeared, and the parents apologized
for their children's behavior.

I learned from this event that I had to lead by example
instead of by sermon, and my people realized that I was
human. I, too, am capable of making mistakes. Most impor-
tantly, the whole experience finally made me realize I was staying in Hawaii. I enjoyed the challenge. I enjoyed the trust that
the residents had in me, and I believed that I could succeed
with my program.

I also knew there was a big reckoning ahead.

Bob and I continued to work as codirectors, but it was getting increasingly hard for me. I put no credence in his philosophy. It hadn't worked in Mendocino, and it didn't work now.
Even though he and Rosie were good people, I doubted
whether they could ever adapt to my ideas of teaching common sense, self-reliance, and responsibility. They tended to
concentrate (which is what they were taught) on lofty, philo-
sophical ideas and goals that didn't make much sense to our
population of teenage dropouts who expressed themselves
mostly in pidgin English.

One afternoon I returned from circuit court to find Bob
running a seminar on Erich Fromm's book, *The Art of Loving*.
I listened for awhile, watching the befuddled looks on the kids'
faces, and it was obvious to me they had no idea what he was
talking about. I interrupted and asked a couple of kids to
explain his lecture, which confirmed my suspicions. I stopped
the seminar and asked Bob to join me in my office.

He yelled, "Vinny, stay out of it when I'm running a seminar. I'll take care of things in the house. You take care of things
outside."

I said, "Bob, you're pontificating and philosophizing to
kids who just don't understand your language. They can't

comprehend what you're saying. You're making them feel inferior, and they're going to split."

We got into a full-blown argument and to settle it, I called an emergency meeting of the board of directors. I told them I had an important point to make. Every ship has only one captain. I said it wasn't up to them to choose. I would either be the executive director, and Bob would work for me, or Bob would be the executive director, and I'd just leave. I told them the residents were our priority, and I didn't think Bob was delivering. I said, "Believe me, I don't want to leave, but he's turning off these kids, and I'm getting tired of patching it up."

For a few minutes there was panic. Then the board decided that Bob and I would each have to write a proposal on what we thought the program, the philosophy, and the goals should be. We were to submit the proposals in one week, and they would make a decision as to who would be the next executive director.

Bob made it easy for me. At the end of the week, he said he was going to submit his resignation and that they would be gone within two days.

That night, after everyone was asleep, I drove to Kailua Beach and walked to my favorite meditation spot. I found the boulder I usually sat on where I could see the shining path the full moon lit on the water. I counted stars and listened to the surf and tried for the thousandth time to resolve the questions in my mind.

Again I thought about the four-and-a-half years I had spent in three of the country's largest and best-qualified therapeutic communities. I knew those experiences would enable me to make some well-informed decisions about what worked and what didn't work.

A lot of garbage was in those programs, but a lot of good as well. For instance, I hated it when Synanon shaved a man's head bald, powdered his skull, and then dressed him up in diapers—degrading him in front of the rest of the family. And I couldn't understand their demand for a commitment to give up your entire life and family and accept the lie that the world was an ocean of insanity and Synanon an island of sanity and that once you step off that island, you would die.

Daytop Village and Phoenix House had things I didn't like too. When Daytop allowed a priest from the Catholic church to run the program, it became too rigid. I hated it when Phoenix House made all the residents sell raffle tickets. To begin with, many of these people were not ready to be on the streets at all. And then, selling raffle tickets was like begging, and the staff gave the residents horrendous quotas to meet.

Sitting there on my rock, I thought about what my own program would be like if I took it beyond its present, primitive state. Naturally, I'd incorporate what I thought was valuable from the programs I'd been in and discard the garbage I didn't like plus throw in some of my own ideas, which I had never been allowed to use before.

Still, the thought of accepting the responsibility for other people straightening out their lives was terrifying. What if I made a mistake as I already had? What if, instead of helping somebody, I actually hurt them? And what if I was wrong— what if I couldn't hack it? Was I setting myself up for another fall, another disappointment?

I had quit using drugs, I had stopped my criminal activities and had learned to respect myself, but could I really teach these things to others? Did I fully realize what the responsibilities of a program director were?

I lit a cigarette and blew the smoke into the warm night air. One part of me was saying, "Hey, Vinny, the hell with all this responsibility and worry." Another part had the adrenalin in my body pumping and had me eager to take on the challenge. Okay kid, I thought, this is your moment of truth. This is the time you prove to Vinny Marino that you've got the guts to do the job.

I walked back to the car and drove home. I woke everybody up, even though it was 2:30 A.M., and told them all of the things that had been running through my mind: my deep feelings, what I was going through, what I had been through, and my decision to go for it. They were elated, excited, and enthusiastic about the thought of a new program. We talked and talked until daylight.

When I awoke, I called Neal and told him of my plans to make our program the finest facility of its kind, anywhere. He became as stoked as I was, and for the first time, I knew I was on my way!

Chapter Four

THE BIRTH OF HABILITAT

T he next day, I called a general meeting in the house and asked all the residents to help me come up with a new name for our program. I explained that I no longer wanted to be associated with Communiversity. The name left a bad taste in my mouth.

Everyone started throwing out names, most with a Hawaiian connotation: Mahalo House, Aloha House, Kamehameha House, and on like that.

I thanked them and said, "Look, I'm not Hawaiian, and I don't think it's proper for me to use a Hawaiian name for a program that is not being run by a Hawaiian."

Finally, someone suggested, "The Habitat," meaning a place to live or dwell, but it didn't spark much enthusiasm.

Then, one of the kids said—and I can't remember his or her name—"How about Habilitat?"

The word struck me just right, and I said, "Hey, I like that." Unfortunately, I was the only one who did. Everyone else was against it. A slight disagreement ensued, and I decided this was a good time to explain that Habilitat was not going to be a democracy. I told them the new name was going to be Habilitat because it was unique, like us. Some people still disagreed, but the name stayed. I also told them that someday the name Habilitat would ring proudly throughout the state of Hawaii and eventually the entire United States.

I telephoned Neal and asked him to set up a meeting with the board of directors in two days. Then I took my proposal, after changing the name from Windward Communiversity to Habilitat, Inc., and had five hundred copies reproduced free, thanks to the Legal Aid Society. My people and I went all over town dropping these proposals off to people and institutions I thought might be interested.

Two days later, we had the board meeting. Neal held up one of my proposals and said, "Vinny, this is illegal. You can't call yourself Habilitat, Inc. You're not incorporated."

I already knew this, but I didn't want to admit it. So I said, "Oh, my god, Neal, I'm sorry. I didn't know. What can we do about it?"

Neal considered for a moment, then replied, "Well, I guess we'll have to incorporate."

I told him, "I'm really sorry I put you guys in this position, but to tell you the truth, I think that's a good idea."

With incorporation, I knew we could get our nonprofit status and apply for a number of grants that weren't available otherwise. We could also attract a lot of tax-deductible contributions from businesses and individuals. So within a short time, we were Habilitat, Inc., with the subtitle "Place of Change."

By now a sort of routine was in place at the Kailua house. After breakfast, we started with a morning meeting. We sang songs and performed spontaneous skits. For example, I'd have some of the troops pretend they were chickens laying eggs. Usually we did something that got a laugh, got the people in an up mood for the rest of the day. But it could also be a lesson in humility. At least once a week, everyone got to play the fool. The morning session worked in other ways, too. Later, in a group encounter session, one of the guys might pull a macho number, but then someone could destroy it by saying, "Hey weren't you a chicken this morning?"

I strove endlessly to generate positive feelings and ideas to keep everyone motivated. I talked about my ideas, dreams, and aspirations—constantly painting the big picture. Eventually we'd have our own businesses, our own property, and we'd be recognized.

Because I believed so deeply what I was telling them, they came to believe it too. I could actually feel that bunch of unrelated kids from widely diverse backgrounds and ethnic origins begin to pull together as a family. From that time on, we've referred to ourselves as the Habilitat Family. For some of the kids, it was the only family they'd ever known. For others, it was a temporary substitute for a family they loved but couldn't cope with.

I didn't realize it at the time, but I had embraced one of Hawaii's ancient traditions called *ohana*. Ohana means the extended family. Years ago, when people couldn't care for their own children for any reason—sickness, economy, the death of a spouse, whatever—they would farm their kids out to a family more able to provide for them. For all of us, the Habilitat Family was ohana, a loving and supportive group at a time when we needed it most.

Of course, it wasn't all sweetness and light. One-and-a-

Some of the original residents at Kailua House.

Kailua House residents in seminar with Vinnie.

half bathrooms aren't really enough for forty-four people, which is how many we had under one roof. Sleeping bags and mattresses on hard floors get old fast, especially when someone in the corner needs to use the bathroom in the middle of the night and, in getting there, steps on a dozen sleeping bodies.

Imagine what it was like when someone needed to relieve himself during the day and found himself thirteenth in line. (The seats were *always* warm!) Or imagine you wanted to take a shower and, guess what, you're number thirty-three. Keep in mind, too, that after the third shower in the morning, the water was always *cold.*

The board finally told me I had to do something. There was a potential fire hazard to say the least. So with the help of a minister, Jim Ledgerwood, I obtained three large tents and two smaller ones. We erected them in the backyard and moved thirty of the residents into them.

At the same time, I was working on an idea to drain the pool and fill it with bunk beds that I would shield with an overhead canopy. I figured we could put about thirty more people in that big hole by using double-deck beds. But I hated the thought of losing the pool. It had been a godsend to all of us. When I came home tired and disgusted after something went wrong in court or when someone split, my attitude had an immediate effect on the kids. Within minutes, we would all be depressed and discouraged, feeding on each other's misery.

That's when the pool offered an excellent release and when sixteen-year-old Maria got outside of herself and showed her willingness to share. She was a natural leader, and I counted on her to go along with anything I wanted to try to keep things positive. When I'd come home in a slump, I'd ask Maria for a hug, then lift her onto my shoulder, rush out of the house, and toss her into the pool, clothes and all. Of course, within seconds, someone threw someone else in the pool, and

it went on and on until we were all wet and laughing and had
forgotten our problems.

Many times, I too was thrown in the pool fully clothed,
wallet and all. When you have to teach by example instead of
sermon, you have to go with the flow. Everybody would start
laughing because Vinny, once again, had managed to prove to
be not only a leader but also a human being.

One day a boy named Gary thought he was really slick.
He locked himself in the half-bathroom so no one could dunk
him, but his plan backfired on him. The guys quickly took the
bathroom door off the hinges with screwdrivers, put Gary on
the door, rushed him out and heaved him into the pool. The
funniest part of all was that at that moment Mickey Hummer
chose to pay us a visit to see how we were getting along in *his*
house. He sloshed through an inch of water in the kitchen and
joined in the laughter. He didn't even threaten to evict us.

Though I felt good about the way we were all living and
working together, I wasn't kidding myself that we could keep
things going much longer. But disappointment followed disappointment in our search for a permanent facility, and my need
for more staff members was well past the crisis stage. So I
called a board meeting and asked the members to send me to
New York where I knew I could round up some experienced
people. This was a tough request for them to honor because
we had no money. I still wasn't getting paid myself, but the
board agreed that some of them would chip in to provide
travel expenses. They would also take turns coming over to
supervise the house while I was gone, and Pam agreed to lend
a hand too. I took off for New York, explaining that I'd call two
or three times a day to check on the facility.

When I arrived in New York, I headed for Phoenix House
and looked up an old friend named Gerard DeLisio who was
about to graduate from that program. I told him I was looking

for staff members for my new program and would like to have him join us. I told him honestly that we had no money, but I painted a rosy and promising picture about our financial future. I explained we had a definite monetary commitment from a local foundation that would be coming in within a month to forty-five days. I also told him he could play a large part in developing the program and be in on the ground floor, and we could build it together.

Gerard came to a meeting at my mother's house in Queens, New York, and brought another old friend, Jerry Cousino, with him. Both of them had worked for me at Phoenix House. As a matter of fact, I had inducted Gerard into Phoenix. Our personalities were similar; we both had a good sense of humor, but when it came down to the bottom line, we got things done. Jerry was also a funny guy. His long suit was public relations and fund-raising, and he had the glib tongue that goes along with this work.

I explained what I had been doing for the last several months, and Gerard agreed to come if Jerry would. He seemed worried about the hot weather in Hawaii and wanted some assurance that I'd provide him with an air-conditioned room. With tongue in cheek, I promised them that their quarters most certainly would be air-conditioned. I neglected to mention that they would be living in a tent next to the swimming pool in the backyard.

At the time these two agreed to come with me, they had not officially graduated from Phoenix House, so we had to break them out and take them to the airport for their departure to Hawaii. The driver of the car was a woman named Vickie Russano, who enters the Habilitat story again a few months later.

I'd known Vickie because she was married to a buddy of mine from my childhood. He was also a resident at Phoenix

House, trying to break his drug habit. Vickie was probably the best female friend I ever had. She drove what we jokingly called, "the getaway car."

When we were safely airborne, and there could be no turning back, I started telling Gerard and Jerry a bit more about their air-conditioned rooms. I waited until we were about halfway across the Pacific Ocean to explain that they would be living in a tent. I hastened to add that it was a nice tent, large and airy, and they would have it all to themselves. There was even a swimming pool beside it, and if they wanted to take a quick morning dip as a refresher, that was fine with me. When I stopped for a breath and looked them dead in their eyes, there was only shocked silence. And then they began to laugh.

We were met at the airport by a group of the residents, who greeted us with signs and cheers. Within a few days, Gerard and Jerry felt right at home. In fact, these two New York transplants worked so well I made another trip to New York and returned with two more old friends, a Puerto Rican named Izmael "Izzy" Carrasquillo and a black kid named Mark Smith. Both were graduates of Phoenix House, and Izzy and I had grown up together.

I have to tell a couple of stories. When I was living on the street, I survived by my wits and imagination—any junkie does—because if you don't learn how to be clever, you don't survive.

Just before leaving on my first recruiting trip to New York I lathered my body with a mixture of iodine and baby oil, which made me look like I had a movie star's tan. When I was asked about it in New York, I said, "You got to be kidding. I only go out in the sun for an hour a week."

Back at the house, another trick brought us food. With forty-four bodies to feed, we were hurting in the supply department. Although some of the local supermarkets were helping, soon we'd have to find another source. I remembered that Synanon always held open houses for the general public, and we started doing the same. We scheduled them for Saturday nights and before our guests arrived, we would hide what little food we had on hand.

When the visitors arrived, I introduced myself and explained to them the plans and goals of Habilitat and candidly answered any questions they had. The evening's finale was a tour of the facility, which ended in the kitchen. We would throw open the doors to our empty cupboards, explaining how sorry we were we couldn't offer refreshments. The cupboard might have one tea bag and the refrigerator—also thrown open as part of the kitchen tour—held perhaps a couple of eggs and a small piece of margarine. I'd always offer them all the water they could drink, however.

It never failed. Every Sunday we were inundated with packages and bundles of food—canned goods, bacon, hams, chickens, furniture, blankets, linens, dishes, silverware.

Such tricks or scams, assured our basic survival. Working through the less physical demons that inhabited the residents' heads took a different and more direct route, usually by playing "games."

Chapter Five

PLAYING GAMES

Maria Lyons was an only child, born on the Big Island but a product of California schools. When she was fourteen, her parents divorced, and she and her mother moved back to Hawaii, where she started smoking pot.

But that wasn't her problem. Her problem was that she was spoiled rotten and on top of that she didn't like herself. At least, that's what I saw right away. I knew something else was there, but that didn't come out until later.

Maria was like a lot of kids I see maybe because of the divorce or the way her parents treated her. That probably made the situation worse anyway. Anything she wanted, she got.

You want a new bike? Okay, darling, you got it. You want a new outfit? Great, have one in every color. Her father was especially loose with his cash, probably out of guilt.

Growing up like this, it's not surprising Maria figured the world owed her a living. When I was a kid, it was different. At eight, I was shining shoes on the street. And I used my hands with the polish instead of a rag because that way I wouldn't use so much polish, and it would last longer. Kids today think life is a free lunch. They lose a tooth, the tooth fairy leaves a dollar, maybe *five* dollars, under the pillow. Christmas time should be the celebration of Christ and a birthday you get a year older, but the way parents run it today, it's "What do you want for Christmas? What do you want for your birthday?" Go to a high school these days, and you can't find a parking place! Every sixteen-year-old kid has a car, and lots are fancier than the ones the teachers drive. When I was sixteen, the only time I had a car was when I stole one. Kids my age were lucky to have a bike.

Anyway, I had met Maria at the Waikiki Drug Clinic, where she was hanging out with other pot smokers and run-aways and—like all the others— was looking for real family, which she didn't have at home. (Her mother worked for a downtown advertising agency, which left Maria alone all day and many evenings.) We talked.

I asked here, "What do you want out of life?"

She shrugged.

I asked her, "What do you want to be?"

She said, "I don't know."

She was lonely, she felt inadequate and insecure, she didn't feel loved. Her story was, sadly, typical.

After a month or two, she said she wanted to come into the program. Her mother agreed, reluctantly, after I assured her that it wasn't her fault, she hadn't *failed*, she just needed some help raising her daughter.

Once Maria was in the Kailua house, she felt like she belonged. She was articulate and very bright, yet she remained unsure of herself. She questioned why people like her because she didn't like herself. Because she was open to talking about such things, she took to the "games" we played easily.

A game is a nondirectional form of group therapy set up to handle behavioral problems. It is a powerful tool in teaching people to get in touch with their feelings, but because of the raw emotions involved, the game sessions must be carefully directed and monitored. I've always insisted that they be held only by me or, when I was able to hire other trained people, by another staff member.

A new resident's first experience with an encounter session usually includes his or her own peer group and a staff member or me. These are called "house games" and are routinely held three evenings a week to discuss house business and to straighten out poor attitudes. It is here that residents like Maria first begin to understand what Habilitat is about.

I'd been in Hawaii for some time before I'd heard the word *ho'oponopono*, which is an ancient Hawaiian process where members of a family get together whenever there's a beef and talk it out. The idea is to keep talking to each other until the conflict has been dissipated and a feeling of peace and harmony returns to the household.

Our household games had the same goal. In such group situations, many individuals learn from others, just by sitting and listening.

The next step is participation in a "special game." These sessions are called by the facility director, staff members, or residents when the conduct of one or more individuals has become disruptive and damaging to the good of the facility. The object of the game is to perform emotional "surgery" on these individuals. We force them to face up to their behavior and modify it to a point where it will be acceptable to their peers and the staff.

Residents playing a game (encounter group), led by Vinnie.

Most important is that the process must do more than just open up the person, it must be skillfully handled so that he or she is also patched up at the end, so the effect of the game will be valuable and positive learning experience and not a destructive one. When I use the words "patched up," I mean the equivalent of what a surgeon does after performing corrective surgery. It is equally important to sew a person up psychologically by putting back all the right parts in the right places and restoring equilibrium.

The only hard and fast rule of a special game or any game is that no one can get up from their chair during the game unless they have permission to go to the bathroom. The chairs are placed in a circle facing inward so each participant can easily see everyone else. The game begins when one person is "indicted" (chosen), either by the group leader or someone else in the circle.

From that point on, the person chosen cannot do or say anything to defend themselves until the game moves on to someone else. This prevents the game from being dominated by the person with the loudest voice or the glibbest tongue. This was one of the modifications I made from what I had learned in prior programs. The one the game is "on" must sit quietly and absorb whatever verbal confrontation occurs. Quickly, everyone's feelings focus on this one individual, and the room resounds with shouted accusations, reproaches, and advice on how that person should change his or her behavior.

Sometimes someone who has a complaint about the way things are going in the house requests a special game, but often, to his or her chagrin, the game works around to where that person becomes the indicted one. When this happens, the individual might hear more than he or she desired, but the process usually results in much emotional and, also, educational growth. It's a good way to teach people to stop whining about their problems and to try handling them themselves. This experience is designed to force self-reflection. That's why I don't allow people to defend themselves against the accusations.

After everyone has had their say, the group leader may allow the person under attack to explain his or her feelings; on the other hand, the leader may not. It's understood that while all feelings are valid they are not always realistic or reasonable. Often people are forced to acknowledge that their feelings could stem from ignorance, perversity, or intolerance—racial or other.

The game can move onto several of the people in attendance. When it's finally over, all the "garbage" is left on the floor, and participants are encouraged to hold no grudges. Usually, afterwards, everyone gathers for a cup of coffee or a snack, and they talk about what went on in their game.

At a later stage of the program, each resident will be included in more sophisticated encounter groups that deal with each person's own "historical pain." These are deeprooted unaddressed problems that are handled in extended encounter sessions or "marathons," lasting from twenty four to forty eight hours with only short breaks. Part of the reason for the length is to exhaust and dissipate the participants' defenses so that they become more receptive to dealing with these deeper issues. Incidents many years old no longer seem to matter to many people, but they are really still lodged deeply in a resident's psychological makeup. Often, these old events are shaping and controlling a person's life.

Maria had been making steady progress in the first couple of months of her treatment, but it wasn't until she experienced her first marathon that she took a big step. Typically, eighteen to twenty five people participate in a marathon, including me and two or three other staff members who've been around long enough to understand and control the process. We're known as facilitators, and it's up to us to bring out the historical pain most people like Maria try so hard to conceal. Our goal is to help each participant face up to and address the crippling emotions that keep them from functioning productively in the present.

Maria joined her fellow residents in the living room where the windows were covered to block all outside light. Incense was burning, and the only illumination came from candles strategically arranged in the center of the room.

I was seated on one side of the room with a staff member opposite me. Maria and the others filled the space between us.

This was to be a one-way game. The game starts with a verbal reprimand to each participant concerning his or her behavior. Bits and pieces of that individual's behavior and attitudes are discussed so the individuals fully understand what's wrong and what part of their daily conduct is holding them back from changing, growing, and becoming emotionally stable. They also learn what's preventing them from being ready to accept the responsibility of managing their lives with logic and common sense. When each staff member, starting with the most junior, has confronted each participant in turn, then I emphasize and embellish what's been said, based on my own knowledge and what I've heard during the session. Before long, a great deal of sobbing and choked emotions break out around the room.

The first segment of a marathon usually takes six to eight hours. Then we have a pause during which we play meaningful message music on the stereo while everyone listens in hushed silence. Over the years, we've found songs like "You've Got a Friend," "Mama," "Daddy's Little Girl," and "He's Not Heavy, He's My Brother" have been effective.

About this time, one or two individuals usually begin to tap into feelings of sorrow, guilt, or fear, commonly having to do with some family member or friend. Most often these responses are tied in with strong feelings directed towards their parents or grandparents. Maybe they feel they let their families down in the past; maybe they feel their families let them down. Sometimes they feel guilty because of what they've put their families through, or they harbor bitter and hostile feelings because of what their families did to them.

These feelings can also relate to siblings or friends. The person might feel guilty about turning on a younger sister or brother to drugs. The guilt could also stem from an incident when the resident allowed a friend to die without trying to save him or let a friend get arrested without warning him. Or, occasionally, he or she could have informed on a friend, who as a result, went to prison.

Conversely, they may be angry because they were betrayed by a friend, spouse, or lover. The possible situations are endless, and I think I've heard them all.

I noticed that Maria began to cry when we played "Daddy's Little Girl." I asked her to please stand up. It was time to use a psychological tool called psychodrama or playacting.

I asked Maria if the song upset her. She nodded that it did.

I asked, "Is it your father?" Again she nodded silently.

"Maria, I want you to look around the room and pick somebody who reminds you of your father."

Slowly, hesitantly, Maria looked at her friends. Finally, she went full circle and came back to me. I wasn't surprised. Usually when people have trouble with their fathers, they pick me—it goes with the job.

I told Maria, "If I was really your father, what would you like to say to me?"

At first Maria said nothing.

"Come on, Maria. Tell me what's on your mind."

At this point, I didn't know what her beef was with her father. It could be any number of things. I knew Maria, like any resident in her position, could be feeling guilt, hostility, ambivalence, any emotion.

Suddenly, she let me have it. For ten or fifteen minutes she did nothing but shit all over me, verbally of course. She told me she hated me for what I did, for taking advantage of her, for using her.

Now I knew. Her father had abused her sexually.

I said, "What is it you want from me, honey?"

That set her off again. For another five minutes she shouted, cried, and shook, abusing me verbally for all the physical abuse she'd gotten when she was just entering puberty.

When she was finally quiet, I apologized. I said I was sorry, and I asked her how I could make it okay.

"What is it you want from me, honey?" I said again.

In a little voice, she answered, "All I want is your love."

I said, "You have to forgive me first . . ."

I hadn't finished my sentence when she looked into my eyes, a mixture of hatred, confusion, and pleading. I went on. " . . . because if you can't forgive me, you can't love me. And I want your love, too. Can you forgive me?"

Maria was silent for a long time, then she wiped away her tears and said she thought she could. As we hugged, I knew she had begun to change.

The process of working on this historic pain can take a long time, but when it is finally accomplished, everybody in the group recognizes that he or she really does belong to the family. They find out they have friends who care deeply about them and will accept them exactly as they are. Everybody is rooting for everyone else in the room to successfully complete the program and take his or her rightful place as a useful, productive citizen.

At this point, we play inspirational music: "God Bless America," "A Place in the Sun," or "I've Got To Be Me." There's much hugging and kissing, as everyone basks in the profound feelings of warmth, affection, and goodwill that the session generates.

The last four hours of the marathon are devoted to hearing feedback from the participants to find out what each one got from the session. Then the game culminates with motivational suggestions from the facilitators to the group. This reinforces their good points but also alerts them to stay on top of their bad points.

Then at the end, we all go for a walk on the beach. We explain that as soon as we leave the room, the hugging and kissing and expressing of historical feelings has ended. In everyday life, these residents must learn to function well, even when they experience strong feelings of love, anger, rejection, or guilt. Each one of us has to learn that we have to reserve these feelings for special times—perhaps for more sophisticated encounter sessions or private discussions.

What has really been accomplished in a marathon is that people have aired their deep-rooted and profound historical pain. Then they have granted themselves or others forgiveness, and love and friendship has been established. After an experience like a marathon, it's very difficult for a resident to revert to playing an insensitive, macho role, whether male or female. They know that someone will always be there to confront them and remind them of what took place during the marathon when they were hurting and vulnerable.

I believe that if a marathon is run very professionally, it is the closest thing to a natural high that a person can possibly feel—certainly the closest thing to feeling high on the deepest of drugs that they have ever used in their lives. Many times, I will wait two or three weeks after a marathon, then call the same group back. We'll play a few of the same songs and ask what they have done to correct their attitudes and behavior since the first group. Since everyone knows that this backup session will probably occur, it reinforces their determination to improve their attitudes and behavior.

All the various games are powerful and effective instruments in teaching people to understand and deal with their emotions. Occasionally, however, for people who are seriously disturbed, the game experience can be dangerous.

One time an incident occurred that shook all of us badly. A resident, a large black man who went by the name of Wee Willie, was a Vietnam veteran. Upon completing his tour overseas, he had also done some prison time for a drug and assault charge. One night, immediately following the first marathon session I had attempted, I was in my office talking with Gerard, who was going through some changes himself, thinking about his mother as a result of the group.

All of a sudden, we heard loud, frightening screams and shrieks coming from the living room. We rushed out to find that Wee Willie had become agitated and tried to dive through a closed window. He was hanging halfway through, one arm shoved through one pane, the other arm through another, and his head sticking through the center pane. He couldn't move because he was suspended on jagged shards of glass left in the frame, and was bleeding all over the wall, the floor, and on the grass outside.

The other residents were hysterical. We phoned for emergency help and, in the meantime, tried to stop his bleeding and calm the other kids down. By now, the neighbors were arriving, responding to the noise and the siren, and the whole place was in chaos.

When Wee Willie had been cared for by the ambulance attendants and taken to a hospital, I called a general meeting and we discussed what had happened. I explained that Wee Willie's behavior had evidently been caused by a combination of two things, which resulted in flashbacks. One was his experience in Vietnam, and the other was the fact that he had long used LSD. The flashback was triggered by one of the songs we had played on the stereo.

Willie survived this episode and was sent to a Veterans Administration hospital for further treatment. Later he came to visit us, but several of our kids went through their own terrifying episodes following his, wondering if something similar could happen to them. A few became so upset they decided to leave.

It was always demoralizing when one of the residents left. Because of the nature of the program, we were all close so that no matter who left the others felt as if they'd lost a friend. Some would get depressed, and they'd be tempted to do what they'd done so often already in their young lives — cut and run, split, get the hell out of this place — as if a geographical change would make a difference.

The situation was like being in the trenches during a war. There, every time someone got killed, it lowered the odds of the others making it, or at least they thought so. Here it was the same. The kids would think one particular guy had a lot going for him, really had it made, and then he'd split. They'd think: If *he* can't make it, how can I?

So when anybody came up missing, or openly took a hike, we all felt a sense of loss and maybe a little failure. One time, though, someone splitting turned out to be funny. A boy left one day without telling anyone. As usual, the whole house turned out to search frantically for him. We scoured the neighborhood with no luck, and we were all feeling pretty low. Finally, we gave up and returned home, to find the kid sitting on the roof with a loaf of bread and a jar of peanut butter. We were so relieved we laughed.

~

Chapter Six

A House Is Not a Home

Inever thought I was doing anything wrong when I hustled and conned and scammed to keep Habilitat going, even when I had to stretch the truth or sometimes create elaborate fictions. After all, isn't this what most businesses do when creating or exploiting a market for their products? When a car manufacturer mounts an advertising campaign to convince us we *need* a new model or a fashion designer tells us bell bottoms are out and narrow neckties are in again, aren't *they* running scams? You bet they are.

I believed in Habilitat so strongly that I knew what I was doing, in the name of survival, was not only acceptable but also worthy of praise. I believed in my "product," and I bet I believed in it more than Ford believed in the Mustang or some unknown designer believed in the narrow tie.

Besides, scamming was a part of my nature — something I did so naturally as not to be aware of doing it. Big executives, however, call it "problem-solving." Well that's what it was for me, too, and as soon as I found that it worked as well in my new, straight lifestyle as well as it had when I was on the street hustling the price of a fix, I put my mind to our biggest problem: housing.

The idea was to create a situation that would attract media attention in the hope that someone, somewhere, would come forward to help us find a larger facility. So I visited all our neighbors and asked them to begin complaining to the police department and say that we were making too much noise, then to call the department of health and say that too many people were living in a single-family dwelling, or call the Bishop Estate and complain to them that too many people were living on a leasehold land facility. Maybe, I suggested, they should even call the fire department and tell them that it was definitely a fire hazard to have so many of us living together.

In the beginning, the neighbors didn't want to go along with our request because they really liked us. But after much convincing, they agreed to cooperate. We were without a doubt in violation of the city ordinance forbidding more than five unrelated people to live in a single-family dwelling. Reluctantly the neighbors began making their complaints to the police department, the health department, the fire department, and the Bishop Estate, demanding we be moved from our property.

In Hawaii, much of the residential land is owned by large corporations and leased to individual house owners. In our case, Bishop Estate was the owner of the Kailua land on which Mickey's house sat, and because of the complaints they soon wanted us off the premises. We were also in violation of the health department so there was no way all the complaints could be ignored.

We received many citations and finally an eviction notice from the Bishop Estate. I now had the reason I needed to call my first press conference, and I found the man who could teach me how to approach the media effectively. His name is Dave Braun, and he had had a lot of newspaper and television experience. He had heard about us and showed up at one of our Saturday night open houses to learn more. He was intelligent, articulate, and extremely humorous. He said he wanted to help and was unemployed so I immediately hired him as one of my staff—with no pay of course because we had no money.

He also had a good friend named Eve Drolet who was an editor for one of the small, local Windward newspapers, and she loaned him her van, which she moved onto our property. We ran an extension cord from the house to his electric typewriter, and Dave used the van as both office and bedroom. He acted as public relations man, promotions manager, advertising executive, and incidentally, my secretary. And he was an alcoholic so he enrolled in the program as well.

The news conference was a success, by the way, at least so far as getting a good turnout from the press went. Both Honolulu daily newspapers were there along with the *Pali Press* and all three network television affiliates. My need for a new home got plenty of exposure, and for the next week, contributions of food and so on arrived by the carload—so did some leads on property.

By then we had a large number of people coming to our open houses in response to the flyers Dave prepared and distributed. Claude Duteil, a local pastor, allowed us to use one of the large meeting rooms at St. Christopher's Church for our gatherings.

I was trying harder and harder to garner additional support from the square element ("square" meaning only nonresi-
dents of Habilitat). To do this we formed a group we called the
"Square Game Club," and at our meetings, I would spend
approximately twenty minutes explaining what an encounter
group was about. Of course, in the beginning, this would be
just a modified version of what we actually played in our
games. First I explained the process; then I answered whatever
questions came up from any of the visitors.

We would all sit around in a circle and part of my explanation was, "Okay, now you're not here to help Habilitat. You're
not here to see what we do. You're here to find out if perhaps,
there are some problems—be it marital, business, personal, or
whatever—that we can help you deal with." We really got into
some nitty gritty things. How to deal with each other in relationships and how they could improve communication with
their children by being more honest and open.

After the game was over, I asked for feedback. Most if not
all of the response was positive, and when the squares came
again, they would bring another couple or some friends they
thought might enjoy what we were doing.

At all of these meetings, I usually began by asking people
to tell me their first names and their occupation. One night, a
couple named Jerry and Joan Greenspan attended. When I
asked about his job, he muttered he was an executive.

"What in the hell is an executive?" I asked. After some
hemming and hawing, he said he was a CPA and that he
worked for one of Hawaii's largest corporations in downtown
Honolulu. When I heard CPA, I'm sure my eyes lit up. I know
bells rang in my head because I desperately needed a money
person. Once again, just when I needed someone, it looked as
if the right person had appeared.

Jerry Greenspan came from a middle-class Jewish family

in Brooklyn. A college graduate, he was supremely witty, quick on his feet, terribly bright and opinionated but also extremely honest. He had been through EST, transcendental meditation, and many other types of motivational groups.

He told me, "Vin, I've experienced them all, and I really like where you're at and where I think you're going. I'd like to be part of what's happening. How can I help?"

I asked Jerry and his wife to stay after the meeting, and, over coffee, I explained how desperately we needed the kind of knowledge he had. He agreed to take care of our financial records, and in no time he became a board member.

Soon he was chairman of the board, and he continued in that position for many years. He became one of the people I refer to as a "rabbi." This term has nothing to do with religious affiliation but is Italian slang for someone who is willing to share his or her valuable knowledge generously with others.

Finding Jerry and Dave eased some problems, but we still hadn't resolved our lack of space. I knew we couldn't continue much longer in the Kailua house. Maintaining discipline and keeping everyone busy was taking up all my time. I had no opportunity to polish and refine the structured program I knew was essential for the residents to progress and achieve my intended results. I was putting in twenty-hour days and falling further and further behind all the time. It seemed I'd tried every possible avenue, and each dead end left me more frustrated in my search for suitable housing. Either the houses I saw were too small—moving from a two and a half bedroom to a four, five, or six bedroom wasn't going to help much—or the landlords turned us down. I couldn't believe I'd come this far just to lose it.

Then when it seemed as if there was no hope, one of our board members heard about a beautiful old estate in Kaneohe, a town about four miles away. Included on the estate were a

Two views of the Bigelow Estate in the early days.

large, two-story house with a full basement, two smaller guest cottages, and three other buildings on an acre and a half of land right on Kaneohe Bay. It sounded too good to be true.

The owner, a widow named Mary Ann Bigelow, didn't want to sell the property and was looking for a tenant who would lease it and care for it properly. It had been neglected for many years because she had moved into a new house adjacent to it. When I first telephoned and introduced myself, she told me very firmly that she was not interested in talking to me.

At first, I couldn't understand, but after listening to her, I could hardly blame her when I found she'd had an alarming experience a year or so earlier. She had rented her place to a group who told her they intended to establish a rehabilitation program, dealing mainly with drug addicts. They were, in fact, looking for an isolated spot where they could have sex parties and use drugs and alcohol. She had had a difficult time getting them off the property, and during their tenure, they seriously damaged some of the buildings and let the gardens and the entire property deteriorate into a jungle.

I decided to try another approach. By an auspicious coincidence, Dave Braun's friend, Eve Drolet, was also a friend of Mary Ann Bigelow's. Eve interceded on our behalf and explained that we were a reputable organization in desperate need of a place to live. At Eve's urging, Mary Ann agreed to meet us, and I picked her up and brought her out to see our small facility. On the way over, I told her about our goals and ambitions and urged her to ask any questions she had.

As soon as she arrived, she was impressed with the immaculate condition of the house and yard. She also fell in love with the kids, as they did with her. Of course, before bringing her over, I had many long sessions with all the residents and made sure that they were well dressed. We also timed it so that at our arrival, they would be singing "Bringing in the Sheaves." I explained to her that this was part of one daily seminar.

Soon after our meeting, Mrs. Bigelow gave me permission to look at her property. As I drove down the narrow road leading to it, I knew the location would be ideal for us. The main house sat on a point of land overlooking Kaneohe Bay with an incredible view of the Pacific Ocean. Steps lead to the beach below, and a long pier extended into the water with a covered boathouse at the end. The neighborhood was so quiet I could hear the small waves lapping at the shore.

As Mary Ann Bigelow showed me around, she told me the history of the estate. Her late husband, Lyman Bigelow—a native of Massachusetts who had come to Hawaii in 1911—had designed and built the place.

Lyman Bigelow had discovered the secluded property while on a field trip in 1920, and during the next few years, he acquired the land and constructed his home, called Dreamwood. He cleaned out the dense undergrowth, leaving only the large trees, and he surrounded the buildings with spectacular gardens filled with hundreds of tropical plants he would collect on his travels. The walks and driveways were paved with brick and laid out in symmetrical patterns in the custom of his native New England. He had also built large ponds where he raised imported water plants, Japanese carp, and ducks. Colorful peacocks roamed the grounds in the daytime and nested in the huge monkey pod trees at night. Pigeons, pheasants, and chickens were housed in an aviary, and the greenhouses were filled with every type of exotic orchid, flower, and fern you could imagine.

After Lyman Bigelow died, Mary Ann felt that she no longer wanted to cope with managing the large estate. Besides, she had too many lovely memories there that constantly reminded her of losing Lyman. She decided to move into a smaller house next door where she still resides and from there, keep an eye on the larger property.

On my first visit, I was only able to inspect the large house and get some idea of the extent of the grounds, but I knew I'd found the place I'd dreamed of as a permanent home for Habilitat. I felt sure that Mary Ann was sympathetic to our cause, but she was still understandably apprehensive about letting us move into her lovely home where she had spent so many years.

I couldn't expect her to feel differently after her earlier experience, but I began an extensive campaign to convince her that we'd treat the place as if it were our own. Finally she agreed to talk to the board of directors, and after several meetings, they came to terms on the financial details. Consequently, this benevolent Hawaiian lady not only agreed to lease the property to us for seven hundred dollars a month, but she also gave us an option to buy it.

When we took possession of the property on August 1, 1971, we needed machetes to clear a path from the gate down to the main house. And when we started to inspect the rest of the estate to prepare it for occupation, we realized that—as usual—we had a bigger job ahead of us than we had counted on.

The first unpleasant surprise came when we found one of the guest houses apparently still occupied from time to time by some drug addicts. They would sneak in at night to sleep or shoot dope. The first time we went in there we found a set of drug paraphernalia, or "works," and I immediately had everything locked up. Then I put the building off limits to all but myself, my staff, and a few selected people who were assigned to clean it up. The guest house was filthy, infested with lice and other unwelcome animal life, and there was tremendous structural damage.

Some of the other buildings needed work, too, and the

The Habilitat family in the early days at the Bigelow Estate.

Gate entrance stating that Habilitat is a place of change.

gardens had been neglected for so long we had to hack our way through them. For several weeks, all of us worked steadily to get the place to the point where we could move in. The big house was in pretty good shape with no major problems other than the fact that it was over fifty years old and totally termite ridden.

On the first floor was a small sitting room just inside the front door and a large living room and dining room overlooking the bay. The nearby library had a wood-burning fireplace that highlighted the display cabinets lining the walls. Originally, they had held Mr. Bigelow's collectables from his extensive travels. Also on the first floor was a large kitchen, pantry, and a breakfast room whose windows framed views of the ocean and the small islands of the bay.

Upstairs were two huge bedrooms with full bathrooms, another sitting room, and a small office. The house was built over a full basement with laundry facilities and a storage vault. We were almost overwhelmed with so much space and quickly realized we were going to need a lot of furniture since, at the time, we owned only a few bunk beds, a pile of mattresses, one dilapidated couch, a few chairs, and one old stove for fifty of us.

On the day we moved into the new property, I called a press conference, and we hid our odds and ends of furniture. When the reporters arrived to publicize our move, we showed them a very large rented truck with only our rusty time-worn stove in it. They assumed that was all we had, and we certainly said nothing to correct the impression.

The next day, when the papers, TV, and radio all came out describing our plight, donations streamed in by the hundreds. We still lacked many necessities, though, so I approached a widely known local disc jockey named Hal Lewis, also known as J. Akuhead Pupule or Aku for short. Despite his name, Aku was also a New Yorker from Brooklyn so I felt sure he'd listen to my pitch.

I was completely taken aback when he said, "Look, Vinny, I've seen every con artist, every hustler, every huckster who's come into this town for twenty years, and I've gotten pretty suspicious. You'll have to prove yourself first. Then, I'll help you, but I have to believe in you."

I told him that was fair enough, and in a short time, he became consistently supportive of Habilitat as well as a close personal friend of mine. He had a tremendous audience on all the islands, and he was responsible for the donation of most of our furniture, office equipment, bedding, linen, bunks, cookware, dishes, TVs, appliances, radios—you name it, he found someone to donate it to us. He even brought in a few used cars that came in very handy.

The girls slept in the upstairs rooms, and the boys in one of the guest cottages. A staff member was always on duty at night, and he slept on the couch in the library.

Mary Ann Bigelow offered me the use of one of the bedrooms in her own home, next door, but this arrangement didn't work out. She had a large, unfriendly Doberman pinscher who challenged me every time I tried to enter the house. Many nights, I was needed in the main house until 1, 2, or 3 A.M. and with Mary Ann already asleep, I couldn't get past her dog. Tired as I was, I wasn't about to argue with it so I'd usually trudge back to my office and sleep wherever I could.

This problem was resolved within a few weeks when a woman who came to one of our open houses at our new facility offered my staff and myself the use of a house she owned on Kailua Beach. I thought at first she wanted to rent or sell it to us, but she graciously let us live there without charge. The place became our first staff house, and it was wonderful to have a place to go and relax away from the facility. The house was brand new and right on the beach. It had no furniture, but we were bachelors and didn't need much. We moved in a couple of beds and that was it.

Right after that we had one of our better dramas, however. We never lacked for drama. Every one of us had a drama going on all the time. Where we'd come from was dramatic, and where we were was dramatic—Sometimes too dramatic.

One night a call came in from Frank Cockett who said he was in Salt Lake, not far from Pearl City, with a guy who had dropped out of the program. Frank said this guy was threatening to shoot everybody in the house. It was three in the morning and after hanging up, I tried to wake Gerard, but I couldn't budge him.

At the time I had this red Cadillac convertible. It was a friend's who was in the Navy, and he'd gone away for three months and let me use the car. I was hardly dressed before I was roaring through Kailua and over the Pali to Salt Lake. I double parked the car in the middle of the street, and there's Frank. Frank is Hawaiian and dark, but on this night, he was white and pointing to the backyard.

I tiptoed down the steps. I'd been around long enough to know when I heard the hammer of a pistol click. So I said, "Kimo, it's me, Vinny. I've got to talk to you."

My eyes were getting adjusted to the dark and finally I saw him. He had the gun cocked, pointed at his head. I didn't know what to say. If a guy's going to jump off a bridge, what are you going to say to him—the water's wet? Anything you say, you might turn him off. So I said, "That's a really funny place to put a gun. You could get hurt like that."

He said, "It's too late for me. She broke up with me. She don't want to know me."

I said, "We can work that out later. Why don't you give me the gun because you got neighbors around who might hear."

When he heard me say neighbors, he turned the gun towards me. He said, "What neighbors?"

He was starting to panic. I said, "Nobody's heard you yet. That's why I'm here. Give me the gun, and let me take you back to Habilitat before you wind up either dead or in serious trouble."

So he gave me the gun. Now I'm a convicted felon, and I'm not supposed to carry a gun. So I took the bullets out, and I put them in my pocket and put the gun in the trunk of the car. I drove Kimo back to Habilitat and got him set up. Frank followed along in another vehicle.

Then I went home, loaded the pistol, and walked into the room where Gerard was still sleeping. I stood right by his bed in front of an open window looking out onto the ocean and fired off three rounds. Gerard jumped out of bed, pale white, too stunned to say anything.

I said, "Next time, you son-of-a-bitch, when I say 'Wake up, there's an emergency,' and you stay in bed, it's your ass." And I walked out.

The next drama was entirely different. As we were settling into our new quarters, we turned the former library, which was a large room just inside the front door, into an office for Dave Braun and myself. Little did I know that I was kicking up a furor that would eventually threaten Habilitat's existence, change my status drastically, and completely reorganize the board of directors. It seemed like a simple move at the time, but it has since become known as the infamous throne room episode.

Chapter Seven

CLEANING HOUSE

It started when I received a phone call from Bob Fisher. He and another board member, Jerry Greenspan, invited me to come over to Bob's house for a meeting. I couldn't for the life of me figure out what type of meeting they had in mind, nor did I know at the time that this meeting had been called at the urging of some other board members.

When I arrived at Bob's house, it was obvious to me that both he and Jerry definitely had something on their minds. They asked me to have a seat, and we all fixed ourselves a cup of coffee. After we had gotten comfortable for about five minutes, I said, "Okay, what's happening?"

Jerry started the conversation by telling me that he thought that I had become a "fat cat" in my position as the founder and executive director of Habilitat. Further, they said, my office was much too big and pretentious. They also mentioned the large, comfortable recliner-type chair someone had donated, which I was using behind my desk. In all the programs I was in, every director and assistant director had this type of chair. Aside from being comfortable, it was symbolic. It was the biggest chair in the room. Some people were intimidated by the chair, but everyone respected it, and that was the point.

My board of directors, however, had missed the point. They began referring to my office as the "Throne Room." They also insinuated that perhaps I might be losing my mind or, at the least, my sense of perspective.

I looked at them and laughed. I don't know why. Maybe I was laughing because I thought they were crazy or perhaps it was just a nervous laugh. I said I didn't understand their objections since the room was also used often for large meetings, encounter groups, and seminars as well as marathons. I also explained that it was strategically positioned so I could easily keep my eye on what was happening in the house.

No matter what I said, their minds were made up. They told me they had conferred with the other board members, and they had all reached the same conclusion. I had forgotten where I came from, and as a result, they bluntly told me, they were putting me on probation.

I was astonished and went into a virtual state of shock. I couldn't believe what I was hearing. Habilitat had been in operation for nine months, I was killing myself and being successful at something that everyone had told me couldn't be done in Hawaii. Habilitat's population was over eighty and now, for no justifiable, logical reason, they were going to put me on probation? I felt betrayed.

As furious as I was, I managed to control my temper as I

listened to them. Jerry and Bob were good friends and men I admired. They had also worked hard to help Habilitat succeed. Bob was a psychiatrist who had some experience working in and with therapeutic communities. That part really confused me because I was sure he would understand the significance of the symbolic use of the director's office. Jerry's background, on the other hand, was strictly business and finance, but on previous occasions when I had been at meetings in Jerry's office, I had thought *it* was ostentatious. His company also had a sauna and a huge conference room. The situation was totally outlandish. I was thinking to myself, "How in the hell can this guy have the audacity to fault me?"

I very carefully thought about what they were saying, and then I looked at them and said, "Bullshit! You guys came on board to help give us credibility and to help open some doors. I also asked you to assist me in the area of business so I could develop as an executive director. At the time I assumed that the main reason for a board was to help raise money because we couldn't have gotten through certain doors without their credentials and their names on our letterhead and having them make calls ahead for us.

"However, at the same time, the board definitely wasn't supposed to get involved in the clinical side. Really, guys, let's be honest, none of you really has any idea what the day-to-day operation is like.

"Now you're giving me static over a completely insignificant matter which neither one of you understands. I haven't done anything wrong. I simply chose a strategic place for my office. I also believe that you are entirely overlooking what's been accomplished here."

They both looked startled and appeared sheepish as I continued.

"Let me give you guys a quick story. Not long ago, one of

the residents asked me, 'Vinny, how come you go out and hire people to be your boss when they're volunteers?' He was talking about you guys, my board members. I couldn't give him a logical answer, and—you know what—I'm not even sure I know the answer myself."

At that time, I had a total of ten staff people, including myself. All but two had been recruited from Phoenix House. When I returned to the facility that night, I called a meeting and explained what had happened. I asked for opinions and advice. The consensus was totally in my favor: I should get rid of my board.

It's a good thing I am an avid student of Machiavelli. I'd learned through him to give people a forum to voice their opinions to see if someone could come up with a more logical approach than my own. If that didn't happen, then I already knew what I was going to do.

I explained that although I was in complete agreement with their ideas, if I fired the board, I'd find myself in the same position that Communiversity did when Ima and her staff and residents shaved their heads and announced they were moving to the mainland to merge with Synanon. When they did that, posing for pictures that went into the papers, Communiversity became a laughing stock in Hawaii. Habilitat hadn't been in operation very long, and the Communiversity fiasco was still fresh in the public's memory. People would be inclined to think we were going to be the next ones to shave our heads and exhibit other bizarre behavior. I felt our track record was too short to get involved in a public battle with our board.

As I talked, I realized that probation was only a word, and I decided to go along with the board, but I didn't say anything at the time. I called a general meeting and explained again what had happened. They were also mad, but I felt it was my place to take care of it.

I said, "I brought you this far, and I'm not going to go off half-cocked and blow it. The same things I teach you must apply to myself. This is strictly business and not personal. The board members think they're doing the right thing. Let me figure out a logical way to handle it."

Early the next morning, I phoned my old friend Frank Natale, the codirector of Phoenix House, and asked him to come to Hawaii. I told him I was in trouble and needed him as soon as possible. This was a direct distress signal. I wasn't used to handling everything myself. When I had been at Phoenix House and in other programs before that, I held positions of responsibility, but I always had someone I could go to for advice, someone who knew the ropes. In Hawaii, I was alone and I needed some outside approval, which I felt Frank could give me.

He arrived two days later, and I set up an emergency board meeting in my office for that evening. During the day, I told Frank what was happening.

When the board meeting convened, I introduced Frank and said I'd invited him to get the benefit of his long experience. The board then presented its complaints about my large office and the size of the chair I was using. It didn't take long for Frank to break out laughing hysterically.

"You've got to be kidding," he said, "This man is working countless hours every day. I don't know how in the world he wound up in Hawaii. I'd take him back in a minute and put him on my staff in a key position at Phoenix House if he was willing. I can't tell you how many tapes, how many phone calls, and how many letters we've exchanged while he has been here asking for advice and help. Instead of appreciation for what he has done — and most of you probably don't even know what he has done — you're hassling him. What difference does the size of his office make? Vinny needs this office to hold staff meet-

ings, other types of meetings with his troops, special groups —
whatever. Right now we're having a board meeting in his
office. Where would you like to hold board meetings? In the
kitchen?"

Frank broke down laughing again. I noticed that the
board members were squirming, and nobody was making any
eye contact with Frank or with me. To keep the story short, by
the time the board meeting was over, I was given a raise in pay
and elected chairman of the board.

This set Frank off again, laughing and hollering at the
board members.

"You are literally making this man crazy," he said. "First
you tell him his head and his chair are too big and you put him
on probation because he has an office bigger than the toilet.
Now you give him a raise and make him *your* boss? You're
making *me* crazy, and I just got here."

Frank definitely made his point.

After the throne room episode, I realized that I had to get
rid of some of the troublemakers on the board who were getting in the way of whatever progress we were making. At our
next meeting, I explained to the members that I wanted them
to understand what I saw as their position. Technically they
were not there to wield power. I told them that I was looking
for people who would ask themselves, "What am I doing for
Habilitat?" I emphasized that I didn't want a board that would
only be active once a month, on board meeting nights. I
wanted commitment. I also wanted a board that wasn't continually on my back. I needed board members who would go
out and open doors, bring in some money or "in-kind" services,
and help us keep our books straight. Their duty was to speak
out for us in the community and protect and strengthen the
organization in every way they could. In other words, they
were to function as they would on any board for a profit-

making organization. I added that if they did not concur with my feelings, they should go someplace other than Habilitat.

I concluded the evening by asking four board members for their resignations, explaining that it was nothing personal, just a definite clash in our personalities. I tried to be diplomatic. I said I thought that their continuing on the board would be counterproductive to what I thought Habilitat's goals were. I also told them they were uncommitted because they had done nothing to help Habilitat. They seldom came to meetings except to hassle me, and I didn't want them on the board any longer.

Apparently at least one of these disgruntled exboard members went to a reporter on a Honolulu daily newspaper with the throne room story. The reporter, Mike Keller from *The Honolulu Advertiser*, called me and asked to come out the next day. When he arrived, Frank Natale and I gave him a tour of Habilitat, and, in a day or so, a full-page article appeared, telling about Vinny Marino, Habilitat, and the "Throne Room."

Part of the story was not so flattering. That was when Frank told the reporter his honest feelings about me. He said I had to take a lot of the rap for most of my recent problems. "He got himself in over his head. He's a damned fine clinician, but he's not a public relations man, and he's not a fund-raiser.

"He also resents other people without his background or experience telling him how to run the program. That's a personality trait he will have to learn to overcome. In New York, Vinny always had someone to turn to when he got in a jam. Here, he's on his own. He has to run a program which demands one type of personality of him. Then he has to be able to turn around and communicate what he's doing to the outside world, which takes another kind of personality.

"When he gets in a jam, he reverts to street survival tactics. I don't doubt he's tried to lie his way out of some things, and I don't doubt he's blown off steam at the wrong times. He's obviously made a mess of that up to now, but he will grow into it with time. He has to, or he won't make it."

꩜

Chapter Eight

LIFE IN THE GOLDFISH BOWL

It might seem odd, me sitting there letting my old friend put me down to the press. It isn't, really. One of the big things about Habilitat, or Phoenix House, or life for that matter, is if you're not honest with yourself, if you don't accept honest appraisals when they come your way, you aren't going to make it—just like Frank said. What he said made me sound human, that's all. I had a big mouth and I could learn to control that. The important thing was, I had a good program, too.

In the end, the publicity worked for us, and in the weeks after the story appeared in the *Advertiser*, people came from all over the island to see the infamous throne room and my large chair. What had started out as a dismal experience eventually brought us many new volunteers, including a wonderful nurse who offered her services without charge. It also brought new board members, a tremendous surge of donations (again, thanks to my friend and Habilitat's friend, Aku), and offers of assistance from several doctors and attorneys.

As usual, we needed all the help we could get. We had ninety-two residents in the program at the time (aged thirteen to fifty-one), nine of them in what we called "reentry." This was the last stage of the program, when residents are being polished to return to society.

Vic Modesto was one of them. He had come to Habilitat when we were in Kailua from the Navy base at Pearl Harbor, where he was stationed as an enlisted man aboard a nuclear destroyer. He was about nineteen and the son of a migrant Mexican farm worker in California. At home, Vic had experimented with a number of drugs. His favorite was LSD, and he continued to take it on the weekends while in the Navy. Unfortunately, he began experiencing "flashbacks" while on duty, and his commanding officer had him arrested. He was waiting for a court martial when one of his doctors called me to see if we could help.

I said I didn't know, but we could try, and after several meetings, the Navy assigned Vic to eight hours of menial housekeeping chores on base during the day and to Habilitat at night and during the weekends. This was an unusual arrangement, but when I took Vic before the house in a general meeting, I expected my troops to go along.

I was wrong—very wrong. For almost eight hours, I listened to a majority of the residents tell me why I was wrong. They said they didn't want any part-timers in the program, and they didn't trust him hitchhiking between the base and Habilitat because it gave him time to get loaded and come down before getting back.

One of my guys stood up and said, "He'll make a jerk out of us, Vinny."

My troops had a point. I had no control over most of Vic's day, and with the court martial coming up in two months, it was possible he could end up in the Navy brig, and we'd have wasted our time. Nonetheless I was determined to bring Vic in, and I finally put on my hat and laid down the law.

I said, "Sorry, gang. Remember, this isn't a democracy. He's coming in."

Once I said that, the entire house erupted with the chant we used to welcome new residents: "BOOM-DADA-DADA, BOOM-DADA-DADA, BOOM-DADA-DADA . . ." (A chant it took them an entire week to learn!)

Once in, Vic roared through the first couple of months like a champ. This is when the resident lives in the equivalent of a goldfish bowl, when his behavior, attitudes, and habits are closely observed twenty-four hours a day. There is no privacy, and there are no secrets. We have no private sleeping quarters here—only dormitories.

As the date for the court martial approached, Vic got very nervous. This was understandable, considering he might do time, but as it turned out his doctor and commanding officer both spoke highly of him. Not one time in two months was he late to work or late getting back to Habilitat. The Navy even let me testify, and I said he showed a real willingness to change his life. I also mentioned that Vic had a drug problem that the Navy should've detected a long time ago. In the end, the Navy gave Vic a general discharge under honorable conditions and no time in the brig. That meant he was a civilian again and free to do anything he wanted. He decided to stay in Habilitat's goldfish bowl.

We used the goldfish-bowl concept, by the way, for obvious reasons, but also because we can watch people like Vic carefully and learn what it was that brought them to us. At night, residents were assigned to make runs through the house every fifteen minutes to check the rest of the family, as well as look for fire, vandals, or any other problems.

If a resident is unable to sleep for any reason, they are free to wake up the person in the bed next to them and ask to talk. This information is relayed to the staff members via their night report. It is also brought to the front desk by the person being awakened so that whatever conversation ensued can be discussed.

Next day, a staff member will take that resident aside and ask, "What's happening? Why can't you sleep? What's on your mind? What are you experiencing?" In this way, small problems are solved before they become big problems, and the resident realizes that his or her welfare is of primary concern to all of us.

In every way, it's a highly controlled, structured environment. For many new residents, this can involve extreme culture shock because there are so many "no's." Not even Vic's two years in the Navy prepared him for our long list of tabu activities—a list that started with no drugs, no alcohol, no sex, no stealing, no violence, and no threat of violence. They are also constantly being reminded to "do what you're told."

Every move is carefully observed. This enables us to find out what upsets individuals, what excites them, and what threatens them. We constantly explore and test their attitudes, both positive and negative. Right from the beginning, we teach good working habits and discipline. We show them care, love, and concern, and we constantly emphasize the idea that each person is an important part of the family.

I'll give you an example. If someone used the last of the toilet paper and then left without replacing it, there's going to be a consequence. Replacing toilet paper wasn't that simple a thing at Habilitat then. To do it, a person had to go down to the chief expeditor—the guy in charge—and get a key, then go to the supply closet and take out a roll and lock it again, then return the key, and go back to the toilet and put on the roll. It takes time and effort, but if you don't do that, it shows you're still a selfish creep and not thinking of others. And being a selfish creep is no small thing.

In these early days, several small fish ponds were on the property stocked with expensive Japanese carp that looked like huge goldfish but are called *koi*. I'm not sure how it happened, but word got around that I loved those fish and the worst thing that could happen to a resident was to let one of the fish die.

At the same time, the pumps that regulated the water in the ponds were as rotten as everything else and they'd stop at least once a week. Right away, you'd hear someone shout, "The pumps are down! The pumps are down!" And eighteen residents would jump into the shallow ponds—one for each fish—and bend over at the waist and grab a fish around the middle and start walking in circles around the pond—otherwise the fish would die. In fact, once when one fish appeared to be dying, one of the guys gave it mouth-to-mouth resuscitation.

Now I never even liked those fish, but it *was* funny to watch people who thought they were such hotshots with their pantlegs rolled up, bent over at the waist, taking a fish for a walk. And in some strange way, it taught the troops responsibility as well as humility.

As the weeks passed, Vic had to prove he could handle a job responsibly. In the beginning, quite naturally, his jobs were very menial, much like those he had done waiting for his court martial: sweeping or mopping floors, dusting, cleaning bathrooms, simple landscaping, maintenance, or laundry duty.

All Vic's jobs were overseen by senior treatment residents who not only taught him the actual physical and mechanical work but constantly reinforced the concepts and philosophy that made Habilitat work. When Vic showed he was proficient at his new job, and had a good attitude, he was moved to a more difficult and challenging position. This process was structured to build self-confidence and also to keep Vic, and the others, uncomfortable in the face of constant change.

After Vic had been around a while, he was assigned to the kitchen, but we don't just wave a magic wand and say, "Cook!" First, he was taught to wash pots, pans, and dishes, then to clean up the kitchen. Next he learned to serve meals, and finally he was assigned to assist the breakfast crew. After that, he was made an assistant breakfast cook, and—if he had continued on up the line—he would have been an assistant dinner cook and then, the toughest job, dinner cook. After that he could become the "ramrod," which is the assistant to the boss, and finally the actual department head of the kitchen.

Vic didn't go that route. He was shifted to another department, where he again started working his way up the ladder. It's a long, slow, careful process. If after being taught to do any of these jobs, Vic fouled up, he would hear about it in a game. The teaching and challenge was continuous.

The way Vic saw it, part of his challenge was Frank Cockett. It seemed clear to me that Frank was headed for a good job somewhere down the line as a Habilitat staff member. Vic Modesto apparently saw the same thing in his future, and before long a friendly competition developed between the two.

Both were ready for reentry now. Reentry normally lasted six to nine months and finished the eighteen-month to two-year program. Reentry today is much different from what it was in Habilitat's early years. Now we have a dozen well-established successful businesses where the residents get hands-on vocational training. In those days, we didn't have much going for us in terms of business.

Like everything else, we started small. One of the first

efforts was making sand candles and selling them in front of the Gem discount stores. I liked this project because it was very creative, but it didn't take the brains of a rocket scientist. The residents had a chance to express themselves and didn't have to strain. We also had some good artists. Of course, we had some bad artists, too, and we had to melt down a lot of candles.

Vic wasn't one of the best artists, but he was invaluable to the operation because he could be trusted to take the troops outside the facility to the stores and return with them, as well as the money they had earned.

That's the way it was at first. We sold watermelon slices and sesame bars at rock concerts. When Gem asked us to roast chestnuts for the Christmas season, we said we'd do that. (Although later we changed our minds.) It was real nickle-and-dime stuff, but it helped. Besides we had to start somewhere.

By now, in addition to private donations, we were getting welfare checks for some of the residents who qualified, and we received a grant from the Law Enforcement Assistance Agency (LEAA). Then, totally unsolicited, a Hawaii senator named Duke Kawasaki was able to get an appropriation of $25,000 from the state to enable us to upgrade our kitchen. That was the first time I'd heard this man's name, and I sent him a warm thank-you letter, little knowing that he and I would have much more to say to each other a few years down the line.

That was followed by money from the federal government: Title IV money, Title XVI money, then Title XX money, plus grants from the National Institute on Drug Abuse (NIDA).

I was grateful for all this, but I saw Habilitat getting sucked into the same dilemma I had objected to in other programs. The more money we accepted from the government, the more strings they wanted to put on our operation. As I saw it, running our own businesses would free us, at least partially, from government interference.

We headed into our first year-end holiday season with mixed feelings. Knowing that for many of the kids this would be their first Christmas away from home and family and that they would be feeling homesick, I was determined this was going to be a holiday that none of them would ever forget.

Our acquisitions department had been working for weeks, accumulating donations and gifts from parents and other family members, friends, and local and mainland merchants. These had all been carefully sorted and packaged so that the kid from the wealthiest family received the same number of gifts as the kid from the poorest family.

We also used some of the money we received, augmented by donations from staff members, to buy gifts for the patients in Children's Hospital in Honolulu. We hustled some buses so that we could deliver the gifts in person and sing Christmas carols to the unfortunate kids there and to patients in other hospitals throughout Oahu as well.

We trimmed several trees and when it came to planning our Christmas Eve and Christmas Day dinners, I established a pattern that we still follow at Habilitat every year. We had a traditional Italian celebration, for I, too, was homesick. On Christmas eve, we prepared an elaborate antipasto, spaghetti with crabs and tomato sauce, salad, shrimp scampi, baked clams, and homemade Italian bread. We finished with Italian pastries and Italian ice cream.

The next day, on Christmas, we ate more antipasto, ravioli and lasagna with meatballs, Italian sausage, roast chicken, stuffed mushrooms and artichokes, followed by fruit, pastry, roasted chestnuts, and oodles of tea and Italian coffee. Most of the food was donated from the various Little Italy's in the New

York area, Baltimore, San Francisco, and other cities where relatives of residents and staff families lived.

Everyone was so busy with the Christmas activities and the fabulous meals and gifts, they hardly had time to be depressed.

New Year's Eve, we celebrated Hawaiian style. Fireworks have long been an island tradition on that night. The practice stems from the Chinese belief that if you make enough noise, you can kick the old year in the ass and scare the New Year into being good to you. All of us agreed that we certainly needed a good New Year, and we staged a fantastic display with everything from aerial fireworks to firecrackers, again all donated by generous friends and merchants. We fired the rockets and Roman candles from our beach over the bay, and the bright bursts of red and green and gold reflected in the water until it seemed like we were surrounded by lights.

Noise from the thousands of firecrackers that we exploded nearly deafened us and the neighbors, and the smoke hung in the air like fog. All in all we felt we had given the old year a pretty good boot and the new one a hearty welcome in hopes that it would be kind to us. The main thing was that all our troops got really excited and appreciated our display.

During that first holiday season, I thought back over the year and realized we had made some major strides. I had arrived in Hawaii only a year earlier, thinking I was stepping into a fairly simple job as director of induction for Communiversity, a position for which I had been well trained.

In less than two months, I ended up as the proud possessor of a drug rehabilitation program of my own, a job I had very *little* training for, and in a place where people assured me success was not possible and I knew no one to turn to for help. I realized that if I had known then what I was getting into, I would probably have taken the first plane off the island. It had been an awfully tough year, but in retrospect—when I looked at our new facility—I had to admit to a little pride and satisfaction at the way things had turned out. I was finally starting to get the feeling that maybe, just maybe, all of those other programs I had been involved with were wrong, and I was right.

Chapter Nine

ANATOMY OF A BAN
AND A BUST

During the previous summer, my old friend and fellow junkie Frank Russano had come from New York to join the Habilitat program. He was married at the time to Vickie Russano, the woman who had helped me shanghai my first staff members. Frank had a long history of drug abuse, and he had first contacted me while I was at Phoenix House to ask for help. I encouraged him to enter that program, and while he was there, I often talked with his wife, Vickie, giving her progress reports and encouraging her to support him in his efforts to rehabilitate himself.

Shortly after I came to Hawaii, Frank split from Phoenix House and was back on drugs again within a short time. Vickie threw him out of the house and told him she was going to divorce him. She did, however, agree to help him get started on his trip to Hawaii to enter Habilitat.

At first Frank seemed to do well in the program, and he hoped that he could patch things up with Vickie. I, too, thought the marriage might be mended so I wrote Vickie numerous letters about his progress and encouraged her to come for a visit. At Christmas, Frank was allowed to call Vickie in New York, and he begged her to come for a short vacation. He told her that the Hawaiian sun and surf were just what she needed to get her through the New York winter. I agreed and so did Jerry, Gerard, and Izzy, whom she knew very well. We all told her a reconciliation was a possibility if she would only see firsthand some of the changes in Frank. Finally she relented, arriving in Hawaii on New Year's Day 1972. She had left her eleven-year-old daughter, Lila, in New York with her mother.

Vickie planned to spend only a few days in Hawaii, and she came determined that she would not let anyone talk her into a permanent move. She spent the first day or so getting acquainted with the program and the residents and relaxing on the beach.

By the third day, I asked her to participate in a marathon I was holding. She told me I was insane and that she didn't want any part of it, but I persisted until she agreed.

I knew Vickie had had a hard time with her father, so at the appropriate time—about eighteen hours into the marathon—I asked her to stand up and pick someone who could stand in for her father.

She said, "Look, I know where you're coming from. You think I'm going to pick my father out of this crowd, you're nuts. Yeah, I had beefs with my father. Lots of them. But I don't see how talking about it's going to help."

I didn't say anything for a while. Vickie stood in the near darkness, fidgeting.

"Don't give me that bullshit, Vick," I finally said. "Pick somebody, or I'll pick somebody for you."

She picked Richie Rivera, one of my new staff members, who was another old friend from the streets and Phoenix House.

I told Vickie, "If this really were your father and he was standing here in this room facing you, from a gut level, what would you say?"

Pretty soon Vickie was telling Richie what she didn't like. She struggled to maintain her composure, but within a few minutes, she was screaming at Richie, raging over things that had happened years before—feelings she thought she'd forgotten. Before it was over, she was exhausted and virtually in hysterics. When Vickie was finally drained and silent, I asked her, "What do you want from your father?"

Vickie said nothing at first and then, very quietly, she said, "Your love."

I said, "You have to forgive him first."

Vickie nodded silently. She looked into Richie's eyes and said, "I forgive you. Will you love me?"

After the marathon, Vickie, Gerard, Izzy, Richie, and I went to the beach. We helped her to understand what had happened and talked about it. Later, when Vickie returned to the house, several other people—some of whom had been in the marathon and some who hadn't—joined her and began talking about her experience. The talk turned to their own lives and emotions, and soon everyone was sharing their feelings and thoughts.

Vickie said she had never felt such love and caring, such understanding and acceptance. She left the room and called me at home, and I returned to the facility and joined the group. We talked for a long time about understanding "historical pain"—the trouble people experience with their family, spouses, or old friends. These experiences leave wounds that won't heal until they have been recognized, accepted, dealt with, and forgiven.

When Vickie returned to New York a few days later, she struggled throughout the long trip with the sadness she felt at leaving Hawaii and Habilitat. Though she was glad to be back with her daughter and family and was still convinced her marriage to Frank was over, she found she could not forget that closeness, warmth, and sincerity. Her confused and unsettled thoughts disturbed her to the point that, within a few weeks, she became physically sick. When she recovered, she wrote Frank, telling him she was considering returning to Hawaii for the summer when Lila's school year was finished. She also told him she would consider giving their marriage another try, and she went about getting ready to return to Hawaii.

At the same time, I was having severe trouble with my staff. First I had to fire a couple who had come from a branch of the Mendocino Family in California. They just didn't understand the program. And then I fired five more, all formerly from Phoenix House. They couldn't get the hang of what I was doing either.

Mostly the problem was they wouldn't let go of Phoenix House where residents in the program actually waited on staff people — served them meals in bed and gave them lots of personal service. I didn't like that policy. Although I didn't think you had to treat residents as equals, at least not at first, still you couldn't treat them like servants or slaves either.

This reduced my staff to four: Gerard, Izzy, Richie, and me. We were friends, and they agreed with what I was trying to do, but eventually I came to feel that Izzy and Richie had to go, too. They were playing too hard. They had gotten caught up in Hawaii's lifestyle of beaches, beautiful women, and tons of fun, which is fine, except that I hadn't hired them just to have fun. I was still trying desperately to get Habilitat off the ground.

In early March, when I had enough, I called them in and explained to them that although I loved them dearly I was going to terminate them. What I had in mind and what they had in mind were two very different ideas.

"This is one of the hardest things I've ever done," I told them, "but your lifestyle isn't helping me to set up the type of program I'm looking for. Bottom line is, I have to ask myself do I want to have friends around, or do I want fellow soldiers who're willing to go along with the struggle and help me endure and succeed?"

The parting was extremely emotional. I remember hugging Richie and giving him a kiss on the cheek and then the same with Izzy. I explained to both of them, "I love you, but I've got to do what I've got to do. Unfortunately, it's just not working out."

We remained friends. In fact, Richie returned later when he was having some problems and went through the program as a resident for a refresher. I'm sad that I can't say the same about Izzy; he was found dead in a New York tenement with his head blown off by a .357 Magnum. I've wondered if I had gone just a little bit further whether his violent death could have been avoided. I believe, though, that I tried to do what was best for the program.

Now it was just Gerard and me and the residents, worried that the program was collapsing and that they would be out on their own again. I called a general meeting and explained as carefully and truthfully as I could why I felt my actions were necessary. I also told the residents to remember and cherish the things they had learned from Richie and Izzy and the rest but not to spend too much time feeling bad about their leaving. I emphasized that they all were adults and that this particular job had just not worked out for them.

During this same period, I started having trouble with a faulty disc in my back, and I entered the hospital, leaving Gerard in charge of the facility. He ran the program with the help of some of the older residents while I stayed in touch by phone and held a few meetings in my hospital room.

As time passed, the meetings got a little bit deeper each day. Another guy shared my semiprivate room, and apparently he was not feeling good. As we got into our meetings they turned into encounter sessions and started to get loud.

One day this guy screamed, "What the hell do you think you're running here, city hall? Do you realize that I'm a sick man, that I'm dying?"

He freaked out, and I pushed the red button for the nurse. I was sure the guy was going to have heart failure. As they dragged him, bed and all, out of the room, he continued to scream about city hall, meeting halls, a church, "I'm dying," but the noise faded as they moved him down the hall.

The treatment I was receiving was not working and I was going to have to go for surgery. Of course, I was skeptical of what the doctors had told me, but tests showed I had a ruptured disc in my lower spine. I was in such constant pain that I could hardly function so I finally agreed to have the operation.

I insisted on returning to Habilitat first for two weeks to give Gerard a breather and enable me to find someone to help him. I racked my brains and kept coming up with Vickie Russano's name. Though she'd never taken drugs in her life or been in a rehabilitation program, I felt that because of her experience with her husband and her involvement at Phoenix House, and her experience at Habilitat during her trip—plus basically she was a very sharp lady—she would be able to help and support Gerard while I recovered from surgery. I knew that she didn't plan to return to Hawaii until July, but I was in too much pain to postpone my surgery until then.

So in mid-April, I called and pleaded with her to come out. I told her that I would explain when she arrived. At first she declined, saying that she felt she should wait until Lila finished school in June. I used every argument that I could think of and finally, I just asked her straight out, "Vickie, are you my friend?"

"Of course I am, Vinny."

"Okay, if you're my friend, I need you right now."

Two days later she was on a plane to Hawaii.

I knew in my head that what I was doing was the proper thing, but on a gut level, I really, really believed that I had taken advantage of her friendship. I also realized I needed her desperately. I was having tons of mixed feelings: on one hand, I was saying, "Look Vinny, it's the right thing. She'll make a good female role model. She'll be able to back up Gerard, and she'll be an asset to Habilitat."

Then on the other side, I said, "What a creep you are. Here you are dealing with someone who is probably your best friend, and you're manipulating her." I was caught in a turmoil, but once again I justified it like I always justified it. I did what I thought was best for Habilitat.

Before Vickie got there, things went from bad to worse. My last staff member, Gerard, left. I knew he was uneasy when I fired all the other staff, and he also told me once that he didn't like the feeling that he would always be the number two man at Habilitat. I felt he really wanted to run his own program. So without my knowledge, while I was in the hospital, he removed his personal belongings from his office a little at a time. On the day I returned from the hospital, he was gone.

I was angry at what I considered his lack of consideration. He could at least have waited until I was physically stronger. I returned to work the next day and held a general meeting about Gerard's resignation. Most of the residents really liked

Gerard. He was a hard worker with an infectious personality. With his leaving, they were afraid the program really would close.

"I'm the only staff member left," I said. "What you see is what you get."

I pointed to a tape recorder on the front desk and said, "The only time you need to worry is if a general meeting is called, and when you get here, you hear me saying goodbye on tape. But as long as I'm here, this ship will sail, and it will sail a little better each day than it did the day before."

Everyone seemed to settle down, but I was concerned that some of them might decide to split. Here I was trying to hold it together all by myself again when, suddenly, I got some unexpected support. By now, several people in the program had been around for more than a year and had progressed to the reentry phase. One by one, they stood up and reaffirmed their faith in me and in the program. I could feel the mood changing, and we were back in business again.

The next day, Vickie arrived, and I explained what had happened. I called Frank Natale in New York and asked him to return to Hawaii since I was, once more, deep in trouble. He came as soon as he could, and he met with me, Vickie, and the other eight reentry residents, including Vickie's husband, Frank Russano. I explained that though I was reluctant to have back surgery, I was in too much pain to function without it. I couldn't even think straight. I also didn't want to take any pain killers because of my prior history with drugs. I told them I was afraid I'd blow the whole Habilitat program unless I got my back straightened out.

Frank Natale told the reentry people to just take care of business and stay out of trouble while I was in the hospital. I'd been somewhat apprehensive about giving Frank Russano so much control, but Vickie assured me that she could handle him and that she would help the others run the program. Satisfied, I went back to the hospital and had the back surgery. Frank Natale returned to Phoenix House, leaving Vickie and the reentry people to operate the facility.

The operation, though not completely successful, relieved my pain somewhat, but I soon began vomiting blood, and for several days, I couldn't eat or drink. They then discovered that I had a hiatal hernia and needed additional treatment to stop the internal bleeding. When I was finally able to return home, Vickie and some of the reentry residents took turns caring for me.

From my bed I stayed in touch with the facility by telephone. I knew Vickie and the others were doing their best to keep the shop running smoothly, but I had this weird feeling that something was wrong. I called a meeting at my house with several reentry people, Vickie, and one of the board members. I questioned each of the people involved in running the house, but they each assured me that everything was all right. I almost began to feel that maybe I was unnecessarily concerned when I asked Frank Russano how things were going. He replied sarcastically, "Your house has never run better since it opened." Something in that response told me my premonition was valid, but I still didn't know what was happening.

The next day Vickie told me she had to return to New York soon but that she would be back in the summer with her daughter Lila. I pleaded that I needed her badly now since most of my staff were kids in their teens, and they needed someone older to turn to for support. I was afraid if she returned to New York, she wouldn't come back. But she felt she had been away from Lila too long. Besides, Lila was graduating from elementary school, and she had promised that she would be there.

In the next day or so, I developed phlebitis and had to

return to the hospital. Vickie stayed on for a few days. When she left, she promised me that she would return in the summer. After I left the hospital again, I kept tabs on the facility from my home while I recuperated.

Vickie returned with Lila a couple of weeks later and moved in with her husband.

On July 4, I told her I knew something was definitely wrong. I said I thought it probably involved her husband. She looked scared.

I put the house on a "ban." This is a concept similar to a religious retreat, and it's a tool I use when I feel things are not as they should be. The facility might be getting too loose, or too many minor lapses in discipline might come up, or maybe an overall laxness in attitude takes over. When I start to feel that my troops have forgotten why they are here, I'll use the "ban."

Once the ban is established, everything stops that is not essential to day-to-day operations. Except for medical emergencies, no residents can leave the facility, and no visitors are allowed. Even smiling and unnecessary talking are not allowed. There is no TV, no music, no radio. Work hours are extended from early morning until night and are interrupted only for seminars or games that stress Habilitat's values and philosophies.

Bans are often needed when a number of new residents enter during a short period of time. When they first come in, some are particularly hostile, and one might write, "Fuck Habilitat" or something like that on the bathroom walls. Or maybe someone will steal clothing from the laundry and leave a note, such as "The phantom strikes again!" Eventually, though, during a ban the hostility all comes out or gets worked out or someone splits, and we no longer have a wall writer or a "phantom."

The whole purpose of a ban is to get the residents to realize why they're in Habilitat. During a ban, I remind them that in their initial induction interview they were told the program would be difficult. We work hard, play hard, and learn hard. I use the ban as a reminder of what we're trying to do at Habilitat. If they do not choose to stay under these conditions, they're free to leave and often several do.

I look at it as shaking the tree for dead branches or rotten fruit. We get rid of the people who don't really want to be here but who don't have the courage to leave otherwise. Others, who think they want to leave but really don't, are forced to make their decision. The outcome is that the people who remain are more committed, and they will remember why they are here and what they have to do to stay here.

As days and sometimes weeks go by with a ban, we use encounter groups to weed out lackadaisical attitudes or the deadwood.

When we reach the point where I feel the residents realize their priorities, I call an "amnesty." During this short period, usually forty-five minutes to an hour, anyone can confess to anything with no repercussions. This forgives people for many things they have done that are infractions of the rules—such as, stealing a cigarette or two or maybe even a pack, borrowing someone else's clothes without asking, trying to get high on drugs, bad rapping staff or the program, harboring resentment, anything like that.

If, during the amnesty, I feel the atmosphere is still "dirty," I'll extend the session. During that time, I call on different individuals I suspect are guilty of something. They usually stand up at this point and admit what they did, saying, "I stole extra food," or "Yeah, I tried to get high." If I still don't feel that I've gotten the whole truth, I'll give the entire house a verbal reprimand, otherwise known as a "haircut." I tell them that I know they're still dirty and not being real. Then I send them back to work.

In a couple of days, I call another "amnesty." By this time, they are usually pretty desperate and tired. They've been getting up early, working hard all day, and going to bed late and exhausted. In the interim periods, we hold many grueling encounter sessions and seminars. The more tired they get, the weaker their defenses become. During this second meeting, I tell them that if I don't get what I want from the amnesty, the ban will continue until I'm sure that the house is clean again, even if it means staying on ban for months—if that's what it takes.

Sometimes we only need one or two amnesties. Sometimes we have as many as four before we can eliminate the dirt and clear the air. Eventually one of two things will happen: Either people will give up whatever they are holding on to, or they will split. As soon as I feel that the house is clean again— usually it takes two or three weeks but sometimes it takes four, five, or even six weeks—I remove the ban and then, very gradually, the daily routine returns to normal.

During this particular ban, I declared an amnesty after about two-and-a-half weeks, and the usual minor infractions came to light. But I was certain I wasn't getting all the dirt. For instance, several items like small radios and electric razors were missing, and no one had copped to stealing them. I discussed the situation with Frank Russano and asked him if he thought the residents were fed up with the ban. He answered that a lot more garbage was there to come out. He believed the house was still dirty.

Then, over the weekend, I finally found out what had been keeping me so stirred up. Very late, one of the night men named Toby heard a vehicle pull up on a side street. When he went to check on it, he saw a young resident named Bruce get out of one of our vans and hide something at the side of the tool shed. When Bruce left the area, Toby checked and discovered a set of "works" (drug paraphernalia) and a couple of bags of what looked like heroin. Toby awakened Vic, the reentry resident in charge of the house in my absence, and Frank Russano, who was house coordinator, and told them what had happened.

At that point, Vic should have called me at home, but he didn't. Instead, he took it upon himself to confront Bruce. Bruce vehemently denied any involvement and protested that he was insulted at not being trusted. Vic told him he was obviously lying and that he was busted. Then he called me, and I came over immediately.

I wiped Vic out for trying to handle the situation without me and told him that I had a very strong feeling that Bruce was the key to whatever had been going on in the house. I was sure others, including Frank Russano, were involved. Bruce refused to tell us who they were, and when we continued to question him, he split. Bruce had been referred to us from court with the stipulation that if he left before completing the program, he would be in violation of the terms and conditions of his probation and would be returned to jail.

As soon as he split, I called the cops, but for some unknown reason the police and the probation department allowed him to stay on the streets. After several days of pleading with the police to pick Bruce up, I gathered nine of my biggest, toughest looking guys, and we barged into the adult probation office, demanding to see the chief.

Later this man was to become a good friend, but at the time, I imagine he was pretty upset when we insisted that Bruce be picked up immediately. I explained that otherwise, Bruce would be making a fool of me, Habilitat, and the courts, and our credibility in the community was being jeopardized.

I said I would go the media, the governor, the head of the judiciary, and the presiding judge and tell them adult probation was ruining us. I told him we always had to answer to him for every resident that we took into Habilitat who was "stipulated." By the same token, he should answer to us.

This resulted in a ton of pressure on Bruce, who called me and offered to make a deal. He would give me the information I needed if I would leave him alone. I suggested that we meet and talk. When we did, I told him, "Bruce, you know me. I don't make deals. Just tell me what you know, and then I'll decide what I'm going to do."

After thinking over my offer, he admitted it was him and Frank Russano and two others, Claude and Tommy, who were responsible for bringing the dope onto the facility. He also confessed to being responsible for the theft of the radios, the electric razors, and other things, which they had sold to get drugs. I told Bruce I'd give him a choice: I'd either take him back into the program and shave his head or turn him in to adult probation. He opted for the shaved head. After his, Claude's, and Tommy's heads had all been shaved, I brought them all into my office and sent for Frank. Vickie, Frank Cockett, and Dave Braun and two or three other reentry people were also present when Frank Russano arrived. I told Bruce to tell all these people what he had told me. Claude and Tommy backed him up, but Frank denied the charges and threatened Bruce. I stepped in and pointed out that these people had nothing to gain by accusing him. They already had their heads shaved, and they were going to have to work their way back into the family.

Frank continued to deny his guilt. Since all the others had the same story, though, I told him I thought it was obvious that he was dirty.

Frank still refused to cop, even after Vickie told him that she had been aware for some time that something had been going on. Every night he would leave their rooms with the excuse that he was going out for a smoke and or a snack. The others admitted that that was when they met in a storeroom to shoot dope. I told Frank he could stay at Habilitat under the same conditions as the others, and Vickie promised that she would stand by him if he'd be a man and admit he'd made a mistake.

Frank chose to leave Habilitat, and I still remember watching his daughter Lila follow him to the front gate. Big tears ran down her face as she pleaded, "Are you just going to leave us here like this? We came out here for you."

But he just kept walking.

Chapter Ten

GOOD PR AND WEDDING BELLS

By the end of our first year, the publicity was mostly favorable. Our connection with Ima and the Communiversity fiasco was largely forgotten, and the infamous throne room incident had become what it always had been, a big nonevent.

Our other stories were more favorable. Cec Heftel, later elected U.S. Congressman from Hawaii, then owned a television station in Honolulu, and he became one of our biggest fans, producing a flattering minidocumentary about the program. The governor of Hawaii, John Burns, another supporter, and his wife Beatrice attended our first anniversary luau, along with four hundred other well-wishers, who came despite a tropical storm. We had rock bands play at the luau, and the Rev.

First group to complete treatment and go into reentry.

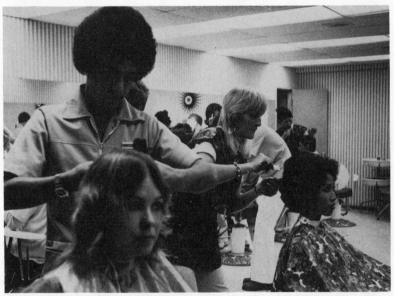

Learning hairstyling skills at the local cosmetology school.

Abraham Akaka was on hand to bless both the facility and our first nine reentry residents.

One significant event I couldn't attend. When I was in the hospital with my back operation, our on-site high school graduated its first eight students. The way we celebrated that first class graduation set the pattern for every time since. We hustled graduation caps and gowns just like those "regular" high school graduates wore. As the "Grand March" from *Aida* filled the air, the eight walked slowly down between the rows of chairs set up outside the house. A light rain was falling as they took their seats in the front row. When their names were called out to receive their diplomas, you could feel their pride.

Afterward they came to visit me in the hospital, and the next day, the newspapers were full of positive stories. It was beginning to look like the establishment loved us.

This wasn't an accident. We courted the press and those in power. We knew we had to have a squeaky-clean image in order to survive. Half of our residents had been referred to us from the courts. More than half had a history of serious drug abuse. So the labels "junkie," "thief," "murderer" were hung on us regularly regardless of the truth. This is a problem every organization like ours has to live with. People say they approve of what we do, but they just don't want us to do it in *their* neighborhood.

For this reason, all through the first year and into the second, we continued to hold regular open houses, inviting not only neighborhood residents but also the public at large to come for a visit, tour the facility, meet the troops. I also made lots of public appearances, and whenever we had an opportunity to take part in some do-good activity, we went for it, just as we had when we sang Christmas carols in hospitals during our first holiday season. Later, when the police department sponsored an island-wide highway cleanup campaign, our people picked up trash along twenty miles of Oahu roadside. Of course we made sure that the newspapers and television stations knew about it.

We also made a big fuss over our first group of people to finish the program. That was on August 27, 1972, a date that nine individuals today remember as clearly as they remember their birthdays. Exactly nineteen months after I'd careened over the Pali in a driving rainstorm to search for a home in Kailua, Habilitat had its first "graduates."

Again we planned a big luau, inviting relatives and friends. More than eight hundred watched as the roll of names was called. Each face glowed with incredible pride, and plenty of cheers and tears welcomed them as they came forward to be recognized.

Frank Cockett got the most attention in the papers, probably because his previous trouble with the law had gotten the most attention too. The headline over one of the stories said, "Former drug user praised in court."

Frank stood before Judge Martin Pence for final sentencing.

"If you had been sentenced nineteen months ago," the judge said, "the odds are very high I would've said, 'The public needs protection from you.' Now it appears that you are on the way to making something worthwhile of yourself and that you are working to make Hawaii a better place in which to live."

Frank, along with Dave Braun, Vic Modesto, Vickie, and one other in the graduating class joined the Habilitat staff. Two others went to work in a dress shop; another became a management trainee at a bank; and the ninth went to work for one of the local radio stations. I was proud.

I did whatever I could every chance I got to keep Habilitat's name in the public eye so that people would hear and read about us and then, maybe, help us. By now our annual budget was way over $100,000, and even with that we were still far short of meeting our operating expenses.

Besides I had new goals. I wanted to buy the Bigelow property, renovate all the existing buildings, and construct some new ones. We were getting static from city and county inspectors and the fire department marshals. They said that we needed more bathrooms, which was certainly true, and that our walls were not structurally sound and we needed another exit as well as a fire escape. I agreed with them, but we had no money to pay for any of these improvements. I couldn't use the operating money I was receiving for capital improvements.

I knew the buildings were old—as a matter of fact, over fifty years old and badly rundown. The walls were paper thin and termite infested. That's why I wasn't too worried about a fire. I figured we could all walk right through the walls if we needed to, and I argued that if the walls were in such terrible shape, what was the sense of going to the expense of building another stairway and exit.

I finally got around this problem by having one of our residents, who was quite artistic, paint a stairway and a door on the outside of the building. When the inspectors came back to take a look at our new stairway and door, they were so impressed with my innovative lunacy that they left the facility laughing and let me get away with it. They knew we were helping many local people so they didn't want to hassle us unduly. They could see that we had cleaned the place up, and everyone was busy all the time maintaining and improving the property. I knew that we wouldn't be able to get away with these stunts after a while, though.

One day the governor's wife, who was confined to a wheelchair, came to visit us, and it became apparent that we didn't have the required ramps to accommodate her chair. Several of the large guys just picked her up gently, wheelchair

The wife of Governor Burns, cutting the lei at the grand opening of Habilitat II.

The Habilitat family at the Habilitat II facility.

and all, and took her up any stairs. This seemed to prove—at least to me—that we didn't need the ramps. We realized, however, that we were going to have to come up with some substantial ideas to take care of our structural inadequacies.

Our fund-raising activities continued, but we weren't able to break into the big time. At one point, I decided to send some reentry people to school to learn a trade we couldn't teach. Three of our males went to a Honolulu school to learn how to be automobile mechanics, and three of the females went to cosmetology school. They weren't particularly thrilled about going out, but they went anyway. Ironically the most trouble they ran into was convincing their fellow students that no, they didn't want to get high.

The experiment didn't work out exactly the way I had thought it would. I had pictured us opening a beauty salon and a gas station or automobile repair shop. It didn't happen. But we did start our own auto shop, where we serviced our vehicles. When the girls started practicing their underdeveloped haircutting skills on the residents right away, the results left something to be desired. Their skills improved with time, though, and when the first young hairstylist finished the course, she went to work with one of the top men in the field in San Francisco.

More successful was our first fund-raising concert, held in January 1973 to celebrate our second anniversary. We held it at the Honolulu International Center, in the Exhibition Hall, which seated twenty-five hundred people. We sold tickets for ten dollars apiece and promised a sit-down dinner with a fantastic show.

We had always been fortunate to have the support of the local entertainment community, and for this concert Ethel Azama, Al Harrington, Danny Kaleikini, John Rowles, the Surfers, Zulu, Jimmy Borges, Rene Paulo, Iva Kinimaka,

Melveen Leed, Nephi Hanneman, Kent Bowman, and many others all donated their talent and time. When it was all over, we netted twelve thousand dollars—not bad considering we didn't know what in the hell we were doing.

At the time, we had seventy-one residents. Even with the big house on the beach and the cottages, it was beginning to feel like the old Kailua house. At night, so many bodies were lying down, we could have filmed one of those crowded hospital scenes in a war movie. We also had the tent up again. We desperately needed more room. Because we couldn't afford to build on the property, we began to search for a cheap, second location.

On February 14, 1973—Valentine's Day—we found it. We moved some of our residents into an old building on the grounds of the Kaneohe State Hospital, which the state rented to us for a dollar a year. The building wasn't in great shape, but it was large. We immediately named our new home Habilitat II. It had two large public rooms, a kitchen, some small offices, plus two long wings, extending on either side. One was the female wing and contained thirteen rooms; the other was for the males and contained eighteen rooms. We used these as bedrooms, assigning two, three, or four people to a room, depending on its size. A long porch or lanai ran across the front of the building, which was situated in a beautiful grassy area shaded by spreading monkey pod trees. No other buildings were close to us so the noise we made didn't bother anyone. There was plenty of outdoor space for volleyball or other games, and the residents could sit and rap under the trees when the work day was finished.

The people I assigned to this building were those who had progressed to the reentry phase of the program and could live with less supervision and handle a little more personal freedom. For a time, we also housed most of our administrative offices there. All Hab II residents still attended games and seminars every week, though, and continued to observe all of Habilitat's rules and regulations.

Before we moved into the building, I asked Mrs. Burns, the governor's wife, to help with the cutting of the traditional Hawaiian *maile lei* at the grand opening. I also asked a Catholic priest, a Protestant minister, a Buddhist priest, and a rabbi to bless the occasion. I wanted to be on the safe side. God knows, we always needed help, and I wanted to make sure I had covered all bases.

It didn't take long to get the Hab II facility bustling, and one day I went to see the administrator of the hospital to ask if we could also use a few acres of vacant land near our building. I said we wanted to plant a garden and I told him that it would be a good learning experience for our residents. In addition, we might be able to provide fresh vegetables for our own use. He seemed pleased by the request and said, "Good, you can use the land on the right side of the road."

I came back with, "What about the land on the left side of the road?" And he said, "Okay, use that, too."

Shortly thereafter I went to the commander of the nearby Kaneohe Marine Corps Air Station and explained my plan to him. He offered to send some of his troops with landscaping and earth-moving equipment. In less than two months, we had a 30-acre working farm, all planted and under irrigation. Eventually, it not only provided much of our food, but we were also able to sell the surplus to the hospital and other community members. As I had hoped, many of our residents learned about farming, crop management, and marketing. The best of this was that we all enjoyed the taste of the delicious fresh vegetables and fruit we grew ourselves.

We did get one complaint, though. After we'd been in business for a while, I got a telephone call from the hospital administrator. He said, "Vinny, I've got a problem. Since you've been operating that farm, the water bill has gone from forty-eight dollars a month to about nine hundred. What's happening?"

I tried to keep from laughing as I replied, "Maybe there's a water leak. You should have it checked."

He wouldn't buy that explanation, naturally, and, of course, we worked out a way to handle our share of the water bill. I couldn't help wondering why the hospital hadn't put this idea into operation long before. It would have been welcome therapy to some of the patients as well as a source of income to the state. In reality, all they would need was one or two experts to teach and oversee the patients.

During this time, I continued to see Vickie socially. She hadn't heard a word from Frank since the day he took his walk. She had filed for divorce right away and decided to make Hawaii her home.

After a couple of months I told her what I really felt. "You know, I think I love you." She thought I was teasing and began to laugh. I told her it was no joke, and I finally admitted that I'd even spoken with Jerry Greenspan and Bob Fischer about my feelings for her. She wanted to know what they said, and I told her they both thought we'd make a great team.

Vickie realized I was serious and said that she couldn't give me a definite response right away. She was still pretty shaken up by her experience with Frank, and she was worried about Lila's reaction too. She also told me she loved me, but she would have to take some time to make a decision about a serious commitment.

In the next few months, we went out once in a while, and I made a great effort to establish a good relationship with Lila. We played, went to the beach, talked a great deal, and I even helped her with her homework. I thought she liked me, but I knew she was still hurting because of Frank's caper.

I asked Vickie to marry me, but she was still worried about Lila's feelings. Now we went out of our way to include Lila when we went places, and one day we took her to the beach and then out for tacos. I explained to Lila that her mother and I had been friends for a long time and now we had grown to love each other more deeply and wanted to be married. Her first reaction was, "Oh, no, not again," and she ran into the ladies' room.

Vickie followed her and explained that nothing was going to happen right away. She said that we would take things very slowly, and if they worked out, fine. If they didn't, we would all still be friends.

Lila agreed, and on January 2, 1973, the three of us found a house and moved in together. Before we made the move, though, we called a general meeting.

I told everybody that I was thirty-four years old and during all my years of drug addiction and lunacy, I had not only never married, but I had never really gotten serious with someone. Some of them had seen me with Pam in the early days in Kailua, but we had gone our separate ways, though we were still good friends, before Habilitat moved onto the Bigelow estate. I had had another girlfriend after that, but more recently the only woman in my life was Vickie. I told the troops that I finally wanted to settle down. I leveled with them about my friendship that had turned into a deep love, and then I announced our engagement. There was tremendous applause. They all stood up and clapped so long I finally had to tell them to stop. Many were teary eyed as they came up and hugged us, and there was so much noise I'm surprised we didn't get arrested.

On June 3, 1973, we were married at Habilitat. The entire facility was decorated with flowers and lush tropical foliage, and Rev. Abraham Akaka, one of Hawaii's most loved and respected ministers, conducted the ceremonies.

Vinny and Vickie, the happy newlyweds.

The wedding party.

At the reception.

Vickie had chosen two graduates of the program as her attendants, and the three of them arrived in a silver Bentley one of the big Waikiki hotels provided. One of the airlines loaned us a black limo for me and my brother Joe, who was my best man. Another airline provided a white limo which carried my mother and my oldest brother Frank. Our staff hustled all of this. We made an impressive procession as we drove onto the facility—something like a Keystone comedy.

We exchanged our vows in front of a beautifully decorated altar set up in front of the main building. Many friends joined the Habilitat staff and residents, standing under the monkey pod tree and crowding around to wish us well when the service was over. Mary Ann Bigelow was bursting with happy tears. In fact, she played her own version of "The Wedding Song" on a piano that had been carried out of the house.

My brother Frank, who has a beautiful baritone voice, serenaded us with several Italian songs. Jimmy Borges, a local Hawaiian entertainer, sang the "Hawaiian Wedding Song." Several other popular entertainers contributed their talents to the reception following the wedding. My brother Frank, imitating Frank Sinatra, and Jimmy Borges, imitating Tony Bennett, sang a touching rendition of "This Love of Mine," which has since become Vickie's and my theme song.

Vickie and I finally drove away in my Volkswagen beetle, the only one on the island with a fancy Rolls Royce hood and grill. I felt so proud and pleased I thought I was going to bust.

A few days later, my mother and brothers returned to New York very happy. Then we honeymooned on the Big Island. Never did a week go by so fast. Too soon it was back to the Habilitat wars, and that's what it was in 1973—war. The Marinos versus the establishment.

Chapter 11

SLINGS AND ARROWS

Two of my heroes are Machiavelli and Saul Alinsky. Machiavelli was an eighteenth-century Italian political theorist who stood for the "haves," who want at least what they've got if not more. In contrast, Alinsky, who was a twentieth-century union organizer, believed in the "have nots" who wanted what was due them.

One of the messages I got from Alinsky came to me in a story about what he did in Harlem. A black guy was walking out of a tenement, and Alinsky asked him how much the landlord paid him to live there. The place was rat- and roach-infested and was painted with cheap lead paint that was peeling; kids would eat it, get sick, and usually die.

The black guy said, "You kidding me, man? He doesn't pay me. He charges me and I pay him!"

Alinsky said, "How can you pay to live in a piece of shit like this?"

The guy said, "Because if I don't he'll evict me."

Alinsky asked him how many families lived there, and the black guy answered forty families. Alinsky said, "Well, what if *everybody* decided not to pay? Can he possibly throw forty families out?"

What happened was that through this one guy Alinsky organized all forty families, who said they wouldn't pay rent until the rats and roaches were gone and the paint was changed. The landlord went to court to get those people out, but he lost.

Ralph Nader is an Alinsky-type guy, and he's another of my heroes. When I see something wrong, I want to change it too. That's why I went after the Waikiki Drug Clinic.

The Waikiki Drug Clinic is not the walk-in induction center Habilitat had in Waikiki that carried our name. The Waikiki Drug Clinic was started in 1967 by the United Council of Churches and the Waikiki Ministry. It operated out of a small cottage in the heart of Waikiki and served as a haven for runaways. People—mostly kids—who had experienced a bad drug trip or were living on the streets and had become sick, could go there and receive free medical examinations, blood tests, and simple medication dispensed by competent volunteer physicians.

When I first found out about the place, I thought it was great. It seemed to be providing a much-needed community service. Frightened runaways and sick kids could go there and feel safe. Even the police and ambulance crews brought in kids.

After a while, though, the atmosphere of the clinic changed. A group of selfish and inept volunteers zeroed in on the clinic as a place to pick up young, inexperienced kids, male and female, for sensitivity, encounter, and massage groups.

They were using the clinic as a front for their own self-serving needs. After observing these groups for a short while, I realized I didn't need a college degree to see that they were really exploiting these young kids. Many times the group leaders would invite young kids to their homes to sleep or get a bite to eat. What happened or didn't happen can only be left to one's imagination, but the one thing I knew was that something smelled fishy.

I was determined to change things, but I also knew it wouldn't be easy. I started by attending each group meeting. Every evening during the week, I went to the clinic and sat in with a different group and listened to the nonsense being espoused. After I figured out the bullshit the leaders were trying to run, I would immediately challenge them, a maneuver definitely designed to stir up any group.

Each group leader had a cadre of people who were quite loyal. When you attack the leader, people in the group will usually attack you because they feel you are out of order by questioning their wonderful guru or mentor. Because of all my years "playing" in groups and then running groups, I chose this way to draw attention to the things I felt were out of order. Naturally my strategy didn't make me the most popular person at the Waikiki Drug Clinic.

Finally, in desperation, the people who were running the clinic met with me and told me that they didn't appreciate what I was doing. They said they wanted me to stop because I was disrupting the whole place. I said I wouldn't stop until they in turn discontinued their questionable encounter, sensitivity, and massage groups. I pointed out that too many sexual overtones and innuendos came up in the group discussions, and also these people were unqualified to perform any type of emotional surgery. I said, "They might push some of the kids past the point where they could be controlled or dealt with."

Of course, they tried to exclude me from the meetings, but over the years I had built up some decent relationships at the clinic. Many of Habilitat's residents had been inducted from there. However irritating I was, they knew my opinion could be valid, even if they didn't like it.

Besides, most of the group were open to the public, and they really couldn't keep me out, even if they wanted to. They knew I'd raise a stink that wouldn't go away.

It took two years, but I finally wore them out. They capitulated and eventually no more encounter groups were held at the Waikiki Drug Clinic.

Next I went after bigger game, taking on the Department of Social Services and Housing (DSSH), which operated the entire state penal system, including Oahu Prison, the Youth Correctional Facility known as Koolau, Halawa Jail, Olinda on Maui, the Kauai Community Correctional Center, the Kulani Honor Farm on the Big Island, and the Hawaii Detention Home for Adolescents.

At Oahu Prison (better known as OP) I had a good rapport with the convicts. I had been able to get many out on early parole so they could enter Habilitat. But I wasn't getting them fast enough. The more time I spent talking to the inmates, the more injustice and inefficiency I saw. The situation was so rotten that I figured the system needed a complete overhaul.

One of my ideas was to set up a labor union within the prison in conjunction with an outside labor union. The outside union would supply the convicts with work from private industry—carpentry, cabinetmaking, metalwork, anything they could do inside the prison walls. My ideas was that the convicts would get minimum pay, and half of what they made would go to the state to help defray the cost of maintaining them. The other half would go to their families, thus reducing the welfare and food stamp monies that most families of convicts were forced to use to survive. It seemed like a good deal all around. The convicts would be doing productive work, maybe even learning a trade, and would create some needed cash to reduce prison costs in the process.

The only real obligation the government had in my plan was to screen the material brought into the prison for the convicts to work on, which isn't such a hassle. At that time, we were doing similar projects at Habilitat. We had a business we called Hab-a-Phones, where we processed audio headsets for various airlines. We cleaned and sterilized them and sealed them into plastic bags, and we were paid a small amount for each headset. We also had Hab Utensils, which processed the eating utensils the airlines used. We sterilized them, put them in napkins, and press-sealed them in clear plastic bags under the same kind of agreement. I figured the prison inmates could do a similar type of work as well as we could.

I also suggested that as union members, the prisoners should have a right to stage a peaceful sit-down strike when necessary. And I felt they should have the right to controlled and structured conjugal visits. Maybe that's what elicited the negative reaction I got. But the truth is, I think the plan made too much sense. It was fair, producing results for the prisoners *and* the taxpayers alike, and I think that's what made it go over Ray Belnap's head.

Ray Belnap was then the administrative head of the prison system, and while I was explaining my ideas to him at our first meeting, he—honest to God—fell asleep. I was angry and insulted because I had been working hard on a proposal which I felt would, on top of everything else, alleviate crowded conditions at the prison.

I don't know how much, if any, of what I said Ray Belnap heard. After I woke him up, he kept yawning, but I kept right on talking.

I told him that in exchange for getting a minimum wage, the convicts would have to guarantee that there would be no drugs, no violence, no gambling, no liquor, and no forced homosexuality. If these guys were willing to go along with these conditions, I said, it would make the administration's job much easier. The public would feel better, too, because the taxpayer's costs would be reduced. Even the conjugal visits were justified, I felt, because that would reduce if not stop the forced homosexual activity.

I told Ray that if these guys eliminated all of the contraband and unacceptable behavior, it would help us gain them an earlier parole to Habilitat. And that would ease the prison system's crowded condition—which sounded reasonable to me.

But it was all too simple and logical for inflexible government bureaucracies. I told Ray right then that I was planning to call a news conference to explain how disappointed I was at being poorly treated when I knew I had some good ideas. I also told him that even if he didn't like my suggestions, he should at least have the courtesy to stay awake during our meeting. The creep.

At the news conference, when someone asked for my opinion of Ray, I said, "The man should be a farmer. At least in a job like that he couldn't do much harm. After all, how can you hurt an artichoke's or an ear of corn's feelings? He certainly shouldn't be the head administrator of a prison system that he doesn't know how to run. He doesn't have the respect of his own administration, much less the respect of the inmates. An organization can only run as well as the guy who's in charge."

Ray was not thrilled, to say the least, and in a policy decision he rejected me and Habilitat entirely—which meant he would no longer let me or my staff inside prison walls anywhere in the state to counsel the inmates on *anything*. Really a creep.

I decided if he wanted to go to the wall, so be it. The next day I called the press again, and this time, I said I was going to sue.

Our attorneys filed suit in federal court on May 9, 1973. In the suit, I said Ray Belnap was denying Habilitat equal rights under the law since it permitted other rehabilitation groups inside. I said he was being "arbitrary, whimsical, capricious, and spiteful." Actually, our lawyers said that. What I said doesn't get included in lawsuits, usually for reasons of "good taste."

Of course, Ray Belnap didn't just sit and take it. That night he appeared on the news, and the next day I answered what he said in another press conference. It went back and forth like that for a week, during which time Ray and I never talked in person. Our attorneys talked instead, and on May 16 I was allowed to visit one of the prison inmates who was a member of the Steps to Freedom Foundation, an organization of prisoners and former prisoners that I had included in the lawsuit. Soon after that, when our regular visits to the prison were resumed, I dropped the lawsuit and for all I know, Ray Belnap went back to sleep.

It should be obvious by now that I don't have much time for bureaucrats. You must realize that most people who work on a government level have to settle for mediocrity. They're just not creative and they're not allowed to be. I believe the union plan would have worked, and it's still a good idea.

As the months passed, I continued to take shots and Ray and the system were the target's bull's-eye. Once, when the National Guard was called in to conduct a search of the prisons, I wondered publicly what the hell was going on. Weren't the prison guards capable of handling a routine search for drugs and weapons? Was it possible, I asked, that some of those same guards were responsible for smuggling that stuff into the

WHO THE HELL DOES HABILITAT THINK THEY ARE?

- PUTTING ON FABULOUS BENEFIT SHOWS
- BUYING THEIR OWN PROPERTY
- SPENDING MONEY FOR FANTASTIC GRADUATION PARTIES
- INVITING THE PUBLIC TO LAVISH FREE LUAUS

- SPONSORING A TEEN FAIR FOR PROFIT
- BUTTING INTO THE PRISON SITUATION
- SUPPORTING A PAID STAFF OF 22 PERSONS
- STILL SOLICITING PUBLIC DONATIONS

WE ARE THE LARGEST, MOST QUALITATIVE, MOST SUCCESSFUL REHABILITATION PROGRAM IN HAWAII. WHERE ARE YOU AT?

COMPARE US WITH OAHU PRISON: Find out how many successfully rehabilitated persons have gone through that system at your tax money. Find out their recidivism rate. (Out of 21 persons who have successfully completed our program at Habilitat, all are gainfully employed and none have been arrested or gotten into any trouble.)

COMPARE US WITH KOOLAU, which costs approximately four times as much, all of which money comes from you. Few lifestyles change for the better at Koolau.

COMPARE US WITH METHADONE MAINTENANCE, and don't be misled by the low cost of methadone itself. Find out exactly the total costs for one person per month stabilizing on methadone. (We have 18 of their former clients. They have none of ours.)

AND LOOK AT THESE FIGURES, FOLKS! Compare costs with using heroin addicts. (A lot of our people had used heroin, but what we're talking about here is just the 29 hard-core, criminally involved dope fiends in Habilitat.) An actual using heroin

addict on the streets has to average stealing $300 a day to support a $100-a-day habit. If the 29 persons now in Habilitat who were on heroin were still in the community committing burglaries, armed robberies, car thefts, muggings, etc., it would cost the community $8,700 a day, $60,900 a week, $243,600 a month or $2,923,200 a year. In Habilitat, rehabilitation for the same 29 persons costs approximately $8 a day each.

COMPARE THESE MONTHLY COSTS PER RESIDENT:	
STATE HONOR CAMPS ...$1,424*	
OAHU STATE PRISON.....$1,035*	
KOOLAU (HYCF).............$986**	
DETENTION HOME...........$735**	
HONOLULU JAIL.............$549**	
HABILITAT, INC.............$250***	

* 1972-3 Budget figures quoted in Governor's Budget Recommendations 1973-75 Biennium
Figures taken from SLEPA's **Correctional Master Plan: Vol. 2, p. 210. These figures do not include In-kind nor Cost of Services Rendered by another agency, such as the DOE.
*** Figures for Habilitat, Inc., based on Budget for Fiscal 1974, do not include donated food and goods. Add $100, totaling $350 per resident per month, to include these in-kind costs.
This is your money, and we feel that as people in the community, you have a right to know what's going on around you — and not by bogus conclusions from trumped-up figures.

HERE'S WHAT WE THINK HABILITAT IS:
• Habilitat is the least expensive treatment facility of its kind — private or state-operated — in Hawaii. It is the only program of its kind in Hawaii that has grown substantially. In three short years, we have grown from 6 to 140.
• A drug-free, nonsectarian, live-in rehabilitation program proving it helps screwed-up people change

their lifestyles. It is the most-often-referred program in Hawaii where parents of teenagers heavy into drugs, alcohol, paint or glue can have any real hope for their future. 32 of our residents are under 18 years of age.
• A live-in program that offers real hope to ex-cons as a transitional environment to a crime-free lifestyle. 69 of our residents would be in jail today if they weren't in Habilitat.
• A place where homosexuals of either sex who would choose a "straight" life if they could are given the emotional foundation to make that choice.
• A place where "local" kids can get help without discrimination. More than a third of our population is "local."
ONE LAST POINT — Why does the Department of Education maintain a school program for us on our own property? Simply because we're doing something with people. To date, 44 of our residents have received their high school diplomas here, and we estimate another 15 during the next semester, totaling 59. At Oahu Prison, 21 persons achieved high school diplomas during the same time span.

WHY ARE WE ASKING HOW PEOPLE IN THE COMMUNITY FEEL ABOUT US?

Habilitat is on the threshold of important expansion seeking to become financially self-reliant. We urgently need to know if the community is behind the work we're doing.

WILL YOU RESPOND TO OUR POLL BY WRITING TO TELL US:

| Yes, I support Habilitat and the work you're doing with young people
Comments: ....
....
....
Name ....
Address ....
City................. State .... Zip .... | If you feel like it

and you can afford

it, send us just $1.00

We will put it

to good use. | No, I don't support Habilitat, and here's why:
Comments: ....
....
....
Name ....
Address ....
City................. State .... Zip .... |

PLEASE FILL IN AND MAIL TO HABILITAT, P. O. BOX 801, KANEOHE, HI. 96744—OR PHONE OUR CENTER, 922-2741, TO GIVE US YOUR YEA OR NAY.

PLEASE LET US HEAR FROM YOU. EVERY VOICE COUNTS.

MAHALO, THE HABILITAT FAMILY

THIS AD SPONSORED BY FRIENDS OF HABILITAT

prisons in the first place—and that's why the job was turned over to soldiers with M-1 rifles? Again I was ignored.

Then in February 1974, we bought a full page advertisement in the Honolulu newspapers. The headline read: Who The Hell Does Habilitat Think They Are?

Then I offered some facts and figures comparing Habilitat to the state's prisons.

"Compare us with Oahu Prison: Find out how many successfully rehabilitated persons have gone through that system on your tax money. Find out their recidivism rate. (Out of twenty-one persons who have successfully completed our program at Habilitat, all are gainfully employed, and none have been arrested or gotten into any trouble.)

"Compare us with Koolau, which costs approximately four times as much, all of which money comes from you. Few lifestyles change for the better at Koolau.

"Compare us with methadone maintenance, and don't be misled by the low costs of methadone itself. Find out exactly the total costs for one person per month stabilizing on methadone. (We have eighteen of their former clients. They have none of ours.)

"And look at these figures, folks! Compare costs with using heroin addicts. (A lot of our people had used heroin, but what we're talking about here is just the twenty-nine hardcore, criminally involved dope fiends in Habilitat.) An actual using heroin addict on the streets has to average stealing three hundred dollars a day to support a hundred dollar-a-day habit. If the twenty-nine persons now in Habilitat who were on heroin were still in the community, committing burglaries, armed robberies, car thefts, muggings, etc., it would cost the community $8,700 a day, $60,900 a week, $243,600 a month, or $2,923,200 a year. In Habilitat, rehabilitation for the same twenty-nine persons costs approximately eight dollars a day each."

Compare These Monthly Costs Per Resident:

State Honor Camps $1,424
Oahu State Prison 1,035
Koolau (HYCF) 986
Detention Home 735
Honolulu Jail 549
Habilitat, Inc 250

Why did we run these ads? Partly it was to show how much tax money was going into the state prison system, which I considered a huge waste. More important, Habilitat was on the threshold of expansion, trying to become financially self-reliant, and we urgently needed to know if the community was behind us.

At the bottom of the ad we included a mail-in coupon for people to tell us why they liked us or didn't. We also said, "If you feel like it and you can afford it, send us just $1. We will put it to good use."

Of course we put it to good use—we used it to pay for the ad. This was something we tried again later, and both times we had enough money to pay the bill within two days. Eventually the newspapers raised their advertising rates astronomically, and we stopped advertising. By then, though, most people knew about us anyway. However, in 1974, we were still relatively unknown.

About the same time we ran the ad, the morning newspaper published a story headlined, "Heroin Problem Fades." Federal experts in Washington were saying the heroin problem was over now that government-administered methadone programs were in place.

I knew this was bullshit. I also knew methadone was worse than heroin. Methadone is a synthetic opiate more addictive than heroin and morphine put together. Addicts were swarming to the methadone clinics nationally and so were teenagers. I wrote an angry letter to the paper.

"I am truly disgusted at the apathetic, unrealistic approach to this problem that has ruthlessly destroyed so many of our young people for so many years.

"Can people in these United States be so unaware, so naive, so easily led—a second time? Many years ago, the 'experts' claimed a high rate of cure in morphine addiction. Morphine usage, they reported, had reached a very low ebb. However, they failed to mention the soaring rise in use of the drug that 'cured' morphine addiction—heroin."

I went on to talk about the high cost of the program and the side effects of methadone (constipation, water retention, loss of sexual desire) that accompanied the crippling addiction. The paper published the letter, and for months afterward I took every opportunity to educate the public about methadone.

At that time, the John Howard Association was the agency administering the methadone program in Honolulu. Compared to other methadone programs in the country, they ran a pretty good shop and doled out their poison carefully. But poison is poison.

In support of my case, I had eight of my troops write statements about their own problems with methadone. One of the guys, then a facility director at Habilitat, had been a former methadone patient. He said withdrawal from methadone addiction was torture, more difficult than heroin withdrawal. (Methadone moves into the marrow of your bones, which is what makes it extremely painful.) Another one of my guys said he would rather be back on the street shooting dope than using methadone again.

What did all this accomplish? Absolutely nothing. What I got for my trouble was to have my old friend and former

Habilitat director Neal Winn, now chairman of the Hawaii Medical Association's substance abuse committee, tell me that methadone was wonderful. I might add that as I write this, another twelve years have gone by, and state and federal authorities *still* think methadone is wonderful.

꒰꒱

Chapter Twelve

SURVIVAL TECHNIQUES

More and more our economic survival was becoming dependent on the so-called generosity of various government agencies. Our funding was coming from dozens of sources now, and too many of them were run by unimaginative, nit-picking, I'm-only-doing-my-job bureaucrats.

I'd been talking about self-sufficiency for a long time, and I knew that to teach my troops that *they* had to be self-sufficient made perfect sense. It made the same perfect sense for Habilitat. In fact, by *not* being financially independent, Habilitat was setting a bad example for its residents. The bottom line was, we had to try harder—a lot harder.

We had learned a great deal from our first concert in January 1973. Even so, a year later we had trouble making a decision whether or not to commit to such a big undertaking again.

Because I was being so outspoken, people told me I was creating problems, and I kept hearing that I was biting the hand that was feeding me, which was, to some degree, correct. On one hand, I was accepting money from the state and federal governments, while on the other, I was attacking their institutions. I knew I didn't intend to continue to take their money, and I was too incensed by some of the bureaucratic foul-ups I'd seen to keep my mouth shut. But others told me I was endangering our opportunities to produce successful fund-raisers.

Meanwhile, I felt that as long as I had public support for my campaigns against state and federal incompetence, the people would continue to support our fund-raising efforts too. When we finally made the decision to go ahead, we had only twenty-nine days left in which to do everything if we were going to meet a deadline of January 27, our anniversary date. We gained two more weeks when the closest date we could get at the location we wanted was February 10, a Sunday. We picked a Sunday because that was when most entertainers would be available.

I held a meeting in my office with all my staff to discuss the operation, and everyone advised me not to try it. We hadn't had tickets printed, we hadn't lined up any entertainers or special guests, there were no musicians or sound system, and we had to sell over eight thousand tickets since we had selected the arena rather than the exhibition hall for this year's show.

I listened to everyone. Then I called Irv Weled, a local promoter and friend, and explained our situation to him. He immediately told me I was crazy, that it couldn't be done, to forget about it. With that, my adrenaline started pumping. I felt challenged to prove what I teach, which is what I learned, that "what the mind of man can conceive and believe, it can achieve." I had conceived the idea, and I believed we could achieve it.

I gave the go-ahead to have the tickets printed, and Dave Braun and I started the public relations work. In the evenings, I would go to Waikiki clubs and line up the entertainers to appear. No one turned us down. Within a few days, we had an even greater talent lineup than the one the year before. Our old friends Ethel Azama, Al Harrington, Danny Kaleikini, the Surfers, Zulu, Jimmy Borges, Iva Kinimaka, Nephi Hanneman, and Kent Bowman were back again from the previous year, and we also got commitments from Emma Veary (who was then married to our good friend Aku), Dick Jensen, Carole Kai, and the Harvey Ragsdale Orchestra, plus special guests Jack and Marie Lord and Jim Nabors.

As I was out talking to the celebrities, staff members and older reentry residents lined up musicians and arranged for the sound system, lights, and a piano.

By the time we got the tickets, we had only twenty-four days left to fill eight thousand seats at $3, $4, and $5 apiece. To help promote things, I got the acting governor, George Ariyoshi, to designate the week before the concert "Habilitat Week." This got the entertainers' pictures and lots of stories in the paper, which is a great way to sell tickets.

Because we were staging the show in the arena, no room was available for a sit-down dinner. Besides, we were told we could not sell food anyplace in the complex because the city and county had exclusive deals with their own vendors.

That was okay with me as I hadn't intended to sell anything anyway. My big gimmick was to give food and drinks away free as our way of thanking people who had bought tickets. I assigned two people from our acquisitions department who were real hustlers to get donations. McDonald's, Wendy's, Kentucky Fried Chicken, and Pepsi Cola all came through with tremendous amounts of food and drink, and many other businesses contributed as well. We included their names in our press releases and on our television spots. I figured it was a win-win situation.

We oversold the arena, and the management had to put in extra chairs. They did this happily because they got paid a percentage of the gross.

The U.S. Marine Band was in place, ready to start playing the Hawaii state anthem and the national anthem, and our people were running around, passing out free food and drinks to everybody. All of a sudden the man in charge of the facility came rushing up. His name was Matt Esposito, and he was shouting, "You can't do this! You can't give away food and soft drinks because my vendors are losing money! You've got to stop!"

As humbly as I could, I answered, "Hey Matt, fuck you! Considering what we're paying you, that's your problem! I'm not here to provide for your vendors. I'm here to provide for our friends."

As the man stood there spluttering and so angry he was shaking, the band started playing "Hawaii Pono I." Calmly, I stood up in proper respect.

Next day, when we made our final count, we had sold 8,755 tickets, netting—after expenses—$26,510. I sent out a news release while the show was still fresh in the public's mind. It had started at 2 P.M. and ended at 9 P.M.—seven hours of constant entertainment plus all they could eat and drink free so they had really gotten their money's worth.

I also said that the money was going toward buying our Kaneohe property. That meant Habilitat could have a permanent home of its own and could start a major building program.

Then, as a parting shot, I revealed not only what we'd taken in but also what all our expenses had been. This included 10 percent of our gross to the City and the County of Honolulu for the use of the arena plus payments for their security and their lighting.

A local newspaper reporter who had a bone to pick with Frank Fasi, the mayor of Honolulu, latched onto the story and blew it out of proportion. It became a full feature story.

Matt Esposito called me up and said, "What the hell are you crying like a stuck pig for? Why don't you act like a man?"

I replied, "Look Matt, all I did was explain to the public who supported us, where their money went. I felt they should know that Habilitat, a nonprofit organization just trying to get started, had to give $7,000 of the money we made to the City and County of Honolulu."

He told me that Mayor Fasi was very upset.

I said, "Okay," and hung up. I told my staff what had happened, and one of them looked at me and said, "Vince, I think you've got big trouble now. You don't want to tangle with Fasi."

So help me, just at that moment, a large frame with a proclamation given to me by Mayor Fasi that was hanging on my office wall, fell to the floor with a resounding crash. Shattered glass flew all over the place.

"Oh shit," I said, "It looks like we *are* in trouble."

Sure enough, I soon got a call from Mayor Fasi, and we set up a meeting. Vickie and I went to his office, not really knowing what to expect, but he was very reasonable.

He said, "I understand what happened. You were used. The media doesn't like me, and you were the pawn."

I answered, "Hey, I know that now. Look Frank, you're Italian and I'm Italian."

But he answered, "Wait a minute, I'm Sicilian!"

I said, "Frank, that's even better. You're Sicilian, and I'm

Sicilian. You're a doer, you get things done for the little people. I'm a doer, I get things done, and I'm for the underdog, too. Why don't we form some kind of marriage where we can complement each other in the things we try to do."

He grinned and said, "What! Married to you?" From that day on, we've been friends.

One of the ways he helped us was to make one of his assistants available to show us how to write grant proposals. Grant writing is an art, and many if not most long-term residential programs like ours were surviving on such grants at that time. That meant a lot of competition was fielded for any funds private foundations offered.

The person on Habilitat's staff who wrote those proposals — and performed other financial miracles — was a woman named Dudley Hoolhorst. She was my first "square" employee, and I hired her shortly after we moved to Kaneohe to serve as my business manager.

Dudley was a highly dedicated person and so frugal she could squeeze the buffalo off of a nickel. She would continually wait until the last minute to pay our bills so we could get more interest on the small amount of money we had in the bank. At times, though, she waited too long, and we actually had our phones and electricity shut off. Each time this happened, I patiently explained to Dudley that I wanted her to pay our bills as soon as they were received so we could establish our credibility.

Obviously we were still living hand-to-mouth, and it was long past time to start a proper money-earning business. So far our attempts to get a beauty salon, a service station, and several other operations under way had failed. We didn't have the capital necessary to get started. All our government grant money plus the money we got from welfare or the courts went directly into covering daily operations. What we got from private sources—foundations, personal contributions, and fund-raising events—disappeared like magician's flash paper on repairs to the aging facility or was held aside in the desperate hope that we might accumulate enough to exercise our option to buy the property from Mary Ann Bigelow.

We talked for hours, days, trying to decide which business to get into that would teach the troops a useful trade, make a decent profit, *and* require little or no initial financial investment on our part. Our answer came from Synanon in the form of a softspoken recovering junkie named Ron Barker.

Ron was the national sales manager for Synanon, heading up an ad specialty business there that grossed $6 million a year. This was one of Synanon's fund-raising operations, and he came to Hawaii to expand Synanon's market in the sale of personalized pens, keychains, baseball caps, and a hundred other small items. When he was talking with Thurston Twigg-Smith, the publisher of the *Honolulu Advertiser,* Twigg-Smith asked him how Synanon compared with Habilitat.

"Habilitat?" Ron said. "What's that?"

Ron's salespeople were getting the same kind of question so Ron tracked us down through our induction center in Waikiki, which Vickie was running. He said he wanted to meet me and visit the facility. I said forget it, but I finally agreed, and he and his friend, Wardell Gohlar, and their wives came out and ran a seminar for the troops.

The seminar was a direct pitch for Synanon and included a very flattering movie. I remember that when they left, one of the residents rushed to the front of the room and wrote on the blackboard, "Lucky you stay Habilitat!" It got a big laugh.

I followed Ron, his friend, and their wives back to my office, where we talked. I got the feeling they didn't want to stay with Synanon. We saw each other again socially before they left the islands, and they got to see me at home with

Vickie and Lila. At the time, Synanon didn't offer its people freedom to have a normal family life. Children were raised in a "hatchery." (I swear, that's what they called it, as if children were chickens!) Ron and his wife Glenda had a baby boy then, and they could tell that what we had was more attractive than what they had back in California.

Another thing was that these people weren't being paid a salary for their work at Synanon, and our staff people were. I felt it was important that staff members earn a salary because it developed pride in accomplishment and consequently self-respect as well as financial security.

About a week later, Ron called from California and said he'd like to come to work for me. I told him he could be in charge of the ad specialty department. He and his wife and son and Wardell and his wife arrived in April 1974.

We already had a small ad specialty business, but we were ordering our product from a local printer, who in turn got the product from the mainland manufacturer. This meant paying a middleman, which was cutting our income in half. If a key-chain cost fifty cents from the manufacturer, the local printer added twenty-five cents to the price before he sold it to us. We charged a dollar. But with Ron's contacts, we could buy direct from the manufacturer.

Ron set up the suppliers, ordered samples, and started teaching twelve of our reentry people how to sell. For two weeks, eight hours a day, he held classes in one of the rooms in Hab II. He also arranged some meetings with local salespeople who volunteered to give our people the benefit of their experience.

The third week, they practiced selling products to each other, and three weeks after Ron and Wardell had arrived, my troops were on the street, canvassing shops in Kaneohe.

At first, the rejection was fierce and very hard for my

people to take. That's were the game proved helpful. Every night, we'd have a feedback session to go over the day's experience, share problems and work them out. And each morning, there'd be another meeting, getting the sales teams as positive and confident as possible before starting in again.

In May, we took our ballpoint pens—our first product, with more to come—to some of the neighbor islands. In June, we went to Baltimore.

Baltimore was important to Habilitat at that time. Ed Taubman, a successful real estate man in Maryland, had a son and a daughter in Habilitat. Like many of the parents, he wanted to help any way he could. We wanted to go national with our ad specialties so he found us some inexpensive apartments in a Baltimore suburb, where our twelve salespeople stayed for nearly six weeks.

As orders were written, Vic Modesto, who captained the team, talked to Ed Taubman and others about setting up another facility in Baltimore. There was already one residential rehabilitation program there called Ex-Cell, and for a while we thought we might get together and set up Habilitat East. We eventually dropped those plans, but through Ed and others who made referrals, troubled Baltimore kids continued to come to Hawaii for help.

Back in the islands, Ron Barker organized new departments to handle credit and collections as the novelty orders started to come in at the rate of a dozen or so a day. By now I also had my brother Frank on staff. He came out in July in answer to my desperate plea. I had advertised in the papers for an overall sales manager—someone who would be Ron Barker's boss as well as honcho several other projects we were planning. I hired one, and when he didn't work out, I hired another, who also couldn't handle it. Frank had his own sales company in New York, but when I explained how much I needed him for Habilitat to survive, he moved his family as soon as his daughter finished the school year.

Speaking of family, my own was about to expand. Vickie got pregnant the end of that summer—an event that excited both of us and furthered the images of mother and father that the troops had for us.

All through the summer and autumn months, novelty sales were good. By Christmas I'm proud to say, our troops took orders totaling $900,000. Our percentage of that was minuscule, and after subtracting our overhead, our profit was almost invisible. But profit wasn't the incentive. The main thing was that our troops were learning sales, how to handle rejection, and how to function in the outside world.

Another fund-raising project in 1974 was what we initially called the *Friends of Habilitat Cookbook*. Later we repackaged it as the *Hawaiian Celebrities Cookbook*.

For many years many kinds of organizations had used collections of local recipes as fund-raisers. In Hawaii, several churches and other civic organizations had tried the format successfully and so had a few drug rehabilitation programs on the mainland. But nothing of the sort had been done in Hawaii recently so we made up a list of four hundred prominent island personalities and wrote letters asking them for the recipes to their favorite dishes.

Bank presidents, politicians, journalists, sports people, top entertainers, every category replied. Governor and Mrs. John Burns sent a recipe for "ono potato salad." A Polynesian performer named Tavana told us how to steam fish Samoan-Tahitian style, and Don Ho provided instructions for making a soup with pig's feet and ginger.

We included one hundred recipes, spread over two hundred pages, with pictures of the celebrities. Artist Jean Charlot sent in a recipe for opihi stew; singer Carole Kai, her instructions

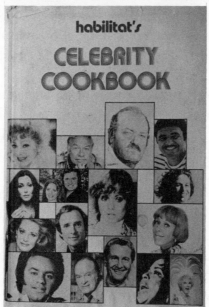

for sweet and sour spare ribs; U.S. Senator Dan Inouye, the "formula" for Vienna Waltz Cheesecake. Other contributions came from Clare Booth Luce for a four-bean pickle salad, Jack and Marie Lord for "Jack's watercress soup," University of Hawaii football coach Larry Price for Portuguese bean soup "Kaaawa style," Mayor Frank Fasi for fried bell peppers, and championship surfer Fred Hemmings for ono fried rice.

I've always believed that promotion was half of sales so we made the names of contributors available to the island gossip columnists and followed that up by releasing some of the actual recipes to newspaper food sections throughout the state. Everyone gave us lots of publicity.

Then the book went into more than a hundred stores, from Sears and J.C. Penney to Carol and Mary and Liberty House. Drugstores, bookstores, hotel gift shops, supermarkets, mom and pop shops—we took it to everyone so that soon the state was saturated. Everywhere you looked, you saw our cookbook. The price was a reasonable $3.95, and we sold twenty-five thousand copies, a staggering number for any kind of book in Hawaii.

Slowly, the tide was beginning to change. In 1974, the year the cookbook was published, we passed the halfway mark on the road to self-sufficiency. In December, Dudley Hoolhurst happily told me that 58 percent of our operating and capital fund budget was now self-generated. Four months later, in April 1975, the figure had moved up to 61 percent.

It wasn't enough, of course, and the overall income figures were not high enough to accomplish all we wanted to. Although we could boast of 54 graduates and another 123 in residence, we had 100 on our waiting list. For them, there still was no room at the inn.

༄

Chapter Thirteen

MOVING INTO THE BIG TIME

T he next three years—1975,
1976, and 1977—were marked by rapid growth. As our population increased to 150, and our annual budget reached $1.5
million, we were desperately trying to come up with new ways
to raise money.

The handwriting was on the wall: We had to do it on our
own because the day was coming when the so-called hand-outs
we were getting from the government and some charitable
agencies clearly would not be there.

One of the first clues came when the state dragged its size
eleven bureaucratic feet in qualifying us to receive food
stamps. We knew our people were entitled because Congress
expanded the food stamp program to include private, nonprofit
institutions offering approved drug and alcohol treatment and

rehabilitation—and we were approved. Congress was very clear; the addicts and alcoholics at Habilitat were eligible.

We still had to go to court to get the state to take any action on the federal rule. We got the usual publicity when we filed our suit. In a couple of weeks, the state came around, and we dropped the suit. To me, it seemed like state harrassment. And even if it wasn't, it was stupid and inefficient and unnecessary.

Then when we got a lot of publicity about how much we were grossing in selling keychains and ballpoint pens, the Aloha United Fund (AUF) got on our case. A local distributor of advertising novelties—one of our competitors—had seen the story and called the AUF to raise holy hell. The distributor was a "member" of AUF, which means the company made a contribution each year. The guy who called wanted to know why he should continue to support the fund when the fund subsidized one of his competitors, Habilitat.

Now the AUF had a rule: no competition. We were not allowed to solicit or compete with any of the members. So it was a catch 22 for us. We agreed to continue to sell specialties for one more year, and the AUF would drop us after 1975. I didn't like to lose the money, but it was only $16,000 at the time, and it wasn't worth all the paperwork and strings attached anyway.

In April 1975, we had our third concert with a bigger lineup of stars than we'd ever had before. After expenses, our net was $42,000—a nice piece of change, but again I was not too happy about how much we had to pay the city and county for use of the Honolulu International Center. As usual, I sent out a press release to announce how much we made and to detail our costs.

I said I thought the city was ripping us off and that I'd complained the year before. At that time Mayor Fasi told me we'd get a break this year, but we didn't.

I said, "What the city is charging us to use this place is ridiculous and outrageous. They shouldn't charge us the same thing they charge profit-making organizations. I don't know much about being a promoter, but I used to be a thief, so I know when I'm being robbed."

We had to give the city 16 percent of our total ticket sales. Over a three-year period, this had cost us $18,000 in fees. When I complained to Matt Esposito—who still hadn't forgiven me for giving food away a couple of years before—he told me to talk to Jim Loomis, who was the information and complaints guy for the mayor. Jim told me to talk to Frank Fasi, and Frank told me it was the city council's decision. When I wrote George Akahane, chairman of the council, he ignored me. I went back to Loomis, and he said if I didn't like the policy, I could take my concert somewhere else.

We decided to make it our last concert, but not for that reason. It just wasn't a challenge any more; and when it stopped being a challenge, it stopped being fun. It also took up a lot of time and effort for the dollars earned. And, to be honest, as grateful as we were for all the free entertainment, some of it got sticky as to who would go on first and who would close the show and who would sing how many songs. It was impossible to please everyone, though we tried.

In every way, 1975 was a year of growth, marked most dramatically by the birth of our daughter, on May 16. We named her Victoria after her mother. Of course we sent out announcements to everyone in the Habilitat family, which by now extended around the world.

"She is beautiful and healthy!" the message said. "Mom is doing fine! Dad is back to *normal*."

When we had found out Vickie was pregnant, I was happy and excited about having a baby. But something bothered me too. I started wondering if all those drugs I had taken would hurt the baby, keep it from growing right. Sure I had been clean for about eight years by then, but I still felt scared. I worried about my child in a way I never did about myself while I was shooting up with anything I could lay hands on. When I saw she was normal, I let out a breath I must have been holding for months.

Things were normal at Habilitat where we had other new arrivals too. They appeared at the rate of three, four, or five residents a week. As always, the drama never stopped even if, at times, it took the form of comedy.

For example, we had a Rose Garden Conspiracy. That came about when Jay Dodson and two other guys who had been in the program for less than three months got together in one of the gardens and began plotting a big drug deal. One of the guys had just inherited $17,000 so he was the "financier" in the group. Jay had done some traveling, had been in Guam once, so they decided he would be the "smuggler." The third guy had local connections so he was going to be the "dealer." The financier would provide the money to send Jay to Guam, then Jay would turn the dope over to the dealer. As they were plotting, a fourth guy happened past, sweeping the walk. He overheard the plans and stuck his head around one of the rose bushes and said, "Count me in for six thousand." And Jay said, "Okay, now we got twenty-three big ones. Let's go!"

They might have pulled it off, who knows? But I doubt it. Instead, Jay changed his mind, and he informed on the other three. Everybody got their heads shaved and started back at square one in the program again.

Another guy found a unique way to get high. We called him the Aqua Velva thief because he'd move around from dorm to dorm, drinking a little out of each bottle of Aqua Velva after-shave that we'd hustled from the manufacturer. He got away with it for a long time until he started stealing from the residents' private stashes of after-shave. We finally figured out who the thief was one day when his breath smelled like Aramis.

Then there was Benny Harrington. He was from Boston and slurred his s's so that he said "shtring beans" and "shmoke a shigarette." We were on a house ban, and during an amnesty Benny wasn't saying anything. Finally, Vickie said, "Come on, Benny, don't you have anything?"

Benny got to his feet and made it one of the longest cop-outs in Habilitat's history. His guilt came, he said, when he had been asked to make a garbage run—take the garbage from the kitchen to the refuse bins. We'd been on the ban for nine-and-a-half days, he went on, and he was allowed no coffee and only one "shmoke" a day.

He said, "I take the gahbage and I walk to the gahbage bin, and it's a long walk to the gahbage bin, and as I'm walking I'm thinking about a shmoke. When I get to the gahbage bin, I dump the gahbage, and I shpot a shigarette butt in the mashed potatoesh."

By now, Benny had been talking for about seven or eight minutes, and everybody's getting bored, wondering when he's going to cop. Vickie interrupted him. "What? What? Come on!"

Benny stopped talking and looked at Vickie and said, "I looked around to shee if anybody was watching, and I took that shigarette butt and I shmoked it, mashed potatoesh and all."

One kid arrived with a whole chest full of stuff—books about black magic that you could tell he had read a thousand times, journals full of mystical writings and strange symbols nobody else could understand, crystal balls, even a god-damned human skull, which I put in my office and used as an ashtray. He told me he was a warlock, a male witch.

An older guy named Joel arrived. He was a dentist from Baltimore who had got himself into trouble by writing himself prescriptions for drugs. His was one of the most memorable interviews. When I got to the point where I told him he was going to lose his wig—which is what we called hair—he smiled, lifted off a very convincing toupe, and handed it to me.

The Bigelow estate was bigger than the house in Kailua by far, but with all these new residents, conditions were just as crowded. In fact, about the same time Victoria was born, we put the tent up again.

The crowded conditions created unusual problems. For a while, we had triple-decker bunk beds at Hab II to put the most people in the least space. This meant the top bunk was about two feet from the ceiling, and residents had to crawl in very carefully. They also had to remember that was where they were sleeping because sometimes we woke everybody up in the middle of the night for a general meeting.

The night man would open the doors and call, "General meeting! General meeting!" And the next thing you'd hear was the sound of people all over the room sitting up suddenly in their top bunks—Boom! Boom! Boom! as their heads hit the ceiling.

The situation wasn't all funny. More bodies meant we needed more money as well as space, and all through 1975, we did everything we could think of to keep the money coming in. We sent our ad specialties sales teams to Atlanta, Tulsa, Kansas City, and Denver and added custom wood plaques to the catalog. (We would glue diplomas, certificates, or photographs on a handsome piece of wood, then lacquer it for hanging on home or office walls.) We reorganized our woodworking shop and started making tikis, benches, tables, and chairs.

After selling 15,000 copies of the *Friends of Habilitat Cookbook* and placing it in most supermarkets and department stores, where it remained a staple for some time, we started collecting recipes for a national version—a 300-page hardcover book that eventually included contributions from Bill Cosby, Cher, Carol Burnett, Hugh Hefner, Burt Reynolds, Steve Allen, Roy Rogers and Dale Evans, Barbara Walters, John Wayne, Phyllis Diller, Ann-Margret, Walter Cronkite, Jimmy Carter, Johnny Mathis, Olivia Newton-John, Bob Newhart, John Denver, Jeanne Dixon, Nancy Reagan, George Peppard, Lucille Ball, Betty Ford, Bing Crosby, and Bob Hope, among others.

It's not fair to pick a favorite recipe, but I will say that the last one in the book was George Burns's "Recipe for Happiness."

"I do not have a favorite recipe, and that is the truth," he said when we asked. "If the food is served stove hot, and there is a bottle of ketchup handy, I am a very happy man."

We started a lawn and garden maintenance service with $700 worth of tools and $106 outlay per month to rent a pickup truck.

We got a local pool-cleaning service to teach some of our re-entry guys their trade, and we started our own pool service with $200 worth of tools and chemicals and another $106 vehicle.

We started selling Christmas trees, soliciting Habilitat's friends with mailers and by phone. The phone number to call: BE JOLLY!

We held a bowling tournament with the military and a tennis tournament with local celebrities. We also sponsored a benefit movie premiere in Waikiki. We put collection cans next to cash registers all over the state: "Why not leave your change for Habilitat—A Place of Change."

We cleaned 100 miles of Oahu's highways in a trash-a-thon, getting local businesses to sponsor us at the rate of $2.50 a mile per resident. We imprinted the business names on the tee-shirts we wore, along with Habilitat's, getting lots of publicity for the sponsor and us. When it was all over, we also recycled more than a ton of aluminum. And, by the way, we sold the tee-shirts from our own tee-shirt factory, another new business.

It all helped, and it kept us in the public eye, but the fund-raiser that gave us the most visibility and the most money wasn't even our idea. Jerry Greenspan and I met with Cec Heftel at his request. He was still running KGMB TV, and he suggested we try a telethon. I liked the idea, but I wondered how we could go on TV for fifteen-and-a-half hours and inspire people to get up from their chairs, walk to a telephone, and call in a pledge to help support Habilitat.

What hook did we have? I could understand why the public would give generously to causes like muscular dystrophy, multiple sclerosis, or Easter Seals, but our kids looked almost disgustingly healthy, and their problems were—in the minds of many people—things they had brought on themselves. I was hesitant to give it a try, but Cec said that he would pay the production costs if we would pay for the air time.

I said, "What if the phones don't ring?"

He said, "Vinny, even if you don't make money, you've got fifteen-and-a-half hours, most of it prime time. You can get your message about Habilitat across to the whole state of Hawaii, plus whatever tourists and visitors in town who watch the show. If you don't reach a break-even point, I'll pay the difference. What can you lose?"

Jerry and I looked at each other, and we could both feel the adrenaline begin to flow. It sounded phenomenal!

However, when one of my board members heard we were doing a telethon, he said, "I don't like telethons!"

I said, "Good. Don't watch it."

Then he said, "You should tell us before you do something like this."

I said, "That's a good point. Next year I'll tell you first."

It wasn't my board's business how I raised money so long

as it was legal. And why, I wondered, wasn't that board member contributing his own fund-raising ideas?

I put Ron Barker in charge of canvassing the business community to line up pledges in advance, just as they did for the Jerry Lewis and other national telethons. (Anybody who thinks the head of McDonald's is sitting at home watching TV and decides to pledge $25,000 on the spur of the minute and shows up at the station half an hour later with a check is nuts.) After a year of selling ad specialties, Ron had left Habilitat, returned to his hometown, Detroit, and had gotten back on junk. He returned again as a resident, and he was anxious to prove himself so I wasn't surprised when he and one other reentry resident got pledges totaling $150,000.

Almost every entertainer in town showed up to perform, and many made emotional pitches for Habilitat. They thanked us for what we'd done for friends they had in the program and for what we were doing for Hawaii. Others said they had friends who needed us.

Mayor Frank Fasi and both U.S. Senators, Dan Inouye and Spark Matsunaga, made endorsements. So did many of our residents and graduates, some of whom told their stories.

My worries about the phone not ringing were unfounded. It rang constantly, and when it was over, collections totaled $178,000. After paying the phone bill and other expenses, our net was $122,000, enough to make a big dream come true.

Our lease with Mary Ann Bigelow was scheduled to expire in June 1976, only three months after the telethon. Just before the deadline, we took the telethon money, along with money from the concerts, the trash-a-thon, and some other events, and exercised our option to buy the place.

When the papers were signed, I took them to the facility and called a general meeting—the most emotional GM in

24 Hour Telethon in 1976.

Habilitat's history. Vickie was by my side as I told the troops, "I have an announcement to make." I tried to keep my voice serious, but I couldn't help grinning.

I held the mortgage over my head and said, "The place is ours! We own it! Nobody can take it away."

The room erupted in cheers and applause. I don't think there was a dry eye as I went on. "The land we're sitting and standing on now belongs to Habilitat. We don't have to worry about getting evicted. We don't have to worry any more about the lease running out. And we did it as a family. A lot of people said we could never do it, and we did it. What the mind of man can conceive, he can do."

Now, I said to myself, all we have to do is conceive of what this place will look like when we get finished with it. I had plans, big plans. I wanted to raze the existing buildings and put up several new ones. It was time to find another money source.

Again the idea came to us—this time in the form of an energetic disc jockey for KKUA, a man who talked so fast it was hard for even me to keep up. Ron Jacobs was an island boy who had just returned after spending almost ten years on the mainland, where he made a big name for himself in rock and roll radio.

Ron told me that he had seen our telethon. When he first tuned in, he said, he expected a piece of shit—a worthy cause, perhaps, but something run by amateurs. What he saw impressed him, he said. It was clear we had our act together, and he had a proposition to make.

Ron said that when he was programming a station in San Diego, he produced several "Homegrown" record albums—albums of original songs written by his listeners, selected in a citywide competition, and used as a station promotion. Now that he was back in Hawaii, he said he was going to repeat the stunt, calling on the rich tradition of island music to produce

the best *Homegrown* album yet. And, he said, he wanted
Habilitat to get all the profits. When I heard what Ron had in
mind, and he told me how he would promote it—and Habilitat—naturally I said yes, promising whatever help he needed.

Our part of the project didn't come in right away. The
first months were all his, as he and the station organized the
contest and promoted it. It was a perfect promotion every step
of the way, and we learned a lot from Ron.

First he announced the contest, talking about it on his
morning show whenever he got a chance. Songwriters and
performers were asked to submit original songs on reel-to-reel
tape. One by one, Don Ho and the names of other celebrity
judges were revealed. With the deadline for entries, the count-
down began. Meanwhile, a second contest was being conducted to find the original album cover art. For this, local
artists were invited to submit their designs.

Day after day, every day, and not just on Ron's show but
on all of the station's shows, around the clock, the "Homegrown" contest was heavily promoted. And *every* single time it
was, Habilitat got a nice plug. Ron's morning show itself was
one of the most popular in the state.

While this was happening, Habilitat was handling the
marketing. We were busy lining up the stores that would sell
the album. Many were shops that already knew us from buying our advertising novelties and other products over the years.
But it was hard to sell sometimes because we were asking the
store owners to buy the albums for $1.69 apiece and then sell
them for the same price.

The idea was unique. Some of the store owners wondered
why we thought they should go to the trouble of inventory and
all that and not make a penny profit. We insisted that with all
the promotion that Ron was giving the project, the album
would create tremendous foot traffic in the stores once it was

available. And that traffic would increase sales generally. This concept took a lot of convincing in some cases — all good experience for the troops in the Habilitat sales department.

Finally, the judges chose the winners, and under a veil of heavy secrecy, the tapes were flown to the mainland where the records were to be pressed. Ron did the interviews with the people in the manufacturing plant, interviews with the people who were going to fly the finished product back to Hawaii, interviews with anybody he could think of.

At last, in October 1976, the first shipment of albums arrived and this is where we came in. Our troops were to provide all the physical labor needed to warehouse and deliver the records to the stores. The way Ron timed it, the first albums went on sale while he was on the air — which allowed him to interview some of the salespeople live and pick up the excitement in the stores.

We knew when we pulled up with the albums that first morning to see *lines* of people outside the stores that we were sitting on a hill of gold. Right away we decided to limit the number of albums to each store, knowing they would run out. We did this to create an even bigger demand, milking the situation for all it was worth.

Next day, Ron was on the air apologizing to his listeners for making some of them wait. More albums had been ordered, he said, and they'd be in the stores shortly. We had them in the Habilitat warehouse, of course, and when the time came, we portioned them out again.

The excitement went on for two months, as Ron continued to promote the album, featuring the twelve winning artists on his show, selling *Homegrown* tee-shirts, planning a television special. Before it was all over, more than fifty thousand albums were sold, an incredible number. Most locally produced albums sold only five thousand copies.

I knew the best deals were win-win deals, where both sides came away happy. This was my first win-win-win-win deal though. KKUA was a winner because it got the audience ratings it wanted, making it the number one rock station. The stores were winners because the free on-the-air promotion that Ron provided and the astounding foot traffic generated more than made up for any work involved. The singers and songwriters were winners because they got their songs and their performances exposed and promoted; many even found jobs and made independent record contracts as a result of the album. And Habilitat was a winner because we got all that good promotion and from every album sold, we got 61 cents (what was left after subtracting $1.08 in costs). By the time all the tee-shirts were sold, the television special was paid for, and a concert was held at the Waikiki Shell, Habilitat netted nearly $53,000.

The next year it was even better. Cec Heftel gave us another fifteen hours of prime weekend television time, and our gross was $256,000, our net $168,000. And again Ron Jacobs produced a *Homegrown* album, which gave us an additional $82,000.

We were on a roll.

Chapter Fourteen

MORE OF THE MARINO MOUTH

As all of this was going on, I continued to shoot off my mouth, ignoring the advice of not only my friend Frank Natale but practically everyone else around me. Actually, I wasn't ignoring my friends. I listened when they spoke. I just decided not to take their advice. I knew being controversial got me in hot water, but I also knew it got Habilitat a lot of public attention. Right from the start, in that little Kailua house, I kept saying that one day Habilitat would be a household word in Hawaii, and speaking my mind was one of the ways I was going to make that happen.

When you go on TV or radio, you have, at most, thirty seconds to get your message across. If I say what a good thing Habilitat is, I come off sounding like Goodie Two-Shoes and nobody's going to remember. Probably nobody's even going to put me on the air. But if I call someone a moron or a jerk, the guy who's sitting there in front of the TV with a beer, he's going to remember me and Habilitat.

Same with the print media. When I talked to newspaper reporters, or wrote a letter to the editor, I said exactly what I was thinking. An example was a letter I wrote the *Honolulu Star-Bulletin* in March 1975. I was reacting to an editorial in the paper commenting on the trial of an inmate who was beaten at the youth correctional facility.

"Congratulations, *Star Bulletin* . . . your March 17 editorial concerning Koolau was so profound I almost threw up.

"The despicable sloth found in Koolau, the stench of urine, the beating up of weaker youths, the mental agony that accompanies a person in Koolau . . . all that is not new. I told you about Koolau long before this trial, and what did I get but a few mumblings and criticism for speaking out.

"Is there even a question about whether the state is responsible for the damage inflicted on one person who couldn't survive in that environment because he wasn't strong enough to fight back? You have the audacity to leave that responsibility up to the courts to decide.

"I can't believe the blindness in this state. Our elected senators and representatives take a tour through the facility and pass on public remarks that liken Koolau to a country club. Have they lost their minds? Would these same officials allow their sons or daughters to spend a summer at the state's youth 'country club'?

"The truth about Koolau is so simple it deceives even our state officials . . . Koolau turns out criminals!"

That wasn't the end of it. A few months later, when an editorial writer for the other paper, the *Honolulu Advertiser*, said Koolau was doing a swell job, I wrote another letter. This time, I urged that the place be shut down. I said it was a tremendous haven for drug use, forced homosexuality and beatings. Besides that, for only 75 residents it was costing the taxpayers $1.2 million a year. I pointed out that Habilitat had 175 residents, and our total operating budget was only $821,000. They were paying their staff more than what our *total* costs were, and we have more than double the residents.

Of course, that was part of the problem: We had too many bodies. For example, we had been housing forty-nine adolescents in a house that we called Hab III. This was a facility I started when some of our older residents at Hab I and II complained about the noise and irresponsible behavior of the children we now had in the Habilitat family. The kids, aged ten to midteens, didn't like living with older people either so I moved them into a house nearby and assigned some of my staff members and reentry residents to supervise the place.

Every now and then I'd drive over, park my car a block away, and make an unannounced visit. Too often I found that the facility was not functioning in accordance with my philosophy. Nothing horrendous was happening, but I quickly realized that I was losing control of the house's operation. In addition, I found we just couldn't afford the extra expense of rent, utility bills, extra staff salaries, and all that so I had to return the adolescents to the main facility.

I tried one other experiment, and it kept me in hot water even though it was highly successful. I began renting homes in established residential neighborhoods and moving small groups of people into them. These were not treatment residents but either staff trainees or residents nearing completion of the program. (Because they didn't require supervision, these houses were less costly.)

In nearly every case, I had asked the neighbor's permission before I did it. Nearly always, however, I ran into resentment and rejection. The standard answer seemed to be some version of, "Yes, I strongly support what you're doing, but, no, please don't do it near my house." I figured we had to be in somebody's neighborhood so I'd go ahead and rent the house. Then late on a Friday night, we'd arrive in a van. We turned the motor off a block away to avoid confrontations. All of our residents wore sneakers, and we pushed the van silently up to our new house. Then we began to unload our furniture and other household goods very quietly. This continued Saturday and Sunday night.

By Monday morning, when the neighbors got up, they were faced with the fact that we had forty to fifty people living in a four or five bedroom house next door to them. Quite naturally, many did not take it well, to say the least. We tried to be good neighbors, and we kept our facilities immaculate, but I'm sure we did make more noise than they had been accustomed to. We were forced by circumstance into this position. Traffic did increase, and a number of people were still firmly convinced that we might go berserk and tear up the whole neighborhood by pilfering, plundering, and raping.

At one neighborhood board meeting I attended I introduced myself, explained our position, and offered to answer any questions from the audience. One woman said, "I don't like what you said about President Nixon in one of your publications."

I replied, as politely as I could, "Look, lady, what does that have to do with us living in your neighborhood?" There was no answer. Then a man said, "I don't like what you said about Spiro Agnew, either."

By this time, I realized that I wasn't dealing with great minds so I just said, "Sir, I've tried to explain our attitude and our position. Now, just let me say, we'll be on call for any of you twenty-four hours a day if you need us. I guarantee your property will appreciate because of the way we take care of our house and property. We intend to be good neighbors, and we hope you'll be the same. If you still want to make trouble for us, it will take you two years to evict us. By then, our building project at Hab I will be completed, and it will be able to accommodate us. At that point, we'll move."

I then thanked everyone for their attention and left the meeting.

In time, we lost all of the smaller homes and were back in Hab I and II. When the adolescents returned, the population of the main house was 106. In Hab II we had 80 people in a complex designed for 25. Crowded conditions like this made me declare a moratorium on placing any more people. In other words, I had to shut Habilitat's doors.

Naturally, I had a solution. I suggested we take over Koolau. My plan was we'd accept all juveniles committed to the Department of Social Services and Housing (DSSH), with the exception of those needing psychiatric hospitalization. The juveniles would first enter a maximum security building staffed by Habilitat graduates. He or she would remain there for thirty days and then would be able to enter Habilitat.

I also said I wanted complete autonomy on program content and use of the Koolau buildings and land. And I said I wanted to fire all sixty-nine full-time state employees then working at Koolau because they didn't know anything about our program.

The state reacted with horror, explaining that these were civil servants and couldn't be fired. They said, "What do we do with them?"

I said, "Give them big hats and horses and make them forest rangers. So what if we don't have any forests. These guys aren't doing anything anyway."

I figured they might say no so I offered an alternate plan

simultaneously. I would take one out of every three juveniles committed by family court and use about half of the total land area and seven of the existing buildings, including the animal farm. The state would retain control of the pool, gym, commissary and chapel, and no one would be fired.

I also presented a fallback proposal where I'd just take over one building, with no commitment to take any additional people from the courts. This was basically an attempt to ease my own population problems.

The state didn't say yes or no. What it did was what bureaucrats usually do when confronted with a good idea: They asked to spend some of the taxpayers' money to do a study. I called a news conference.

I said, "Look, either they're going to give us Koolau or they're not. They should stop horsing around with these studies. The state obviously has fallen down and proved its inability to conduct a rehabilitation program for juveniles or even for adults. All I'm asking for is a pilot program. If we can't produce, we'll back off."

As the arguments went back and forth, Koolau's new director, Vernon Chang, gave an interview to the papers saying that kids at Koolau couldn't handle Habilitat. Chang had worked at Koolau for some time, and he said that of the twenty boys he recommended go to Habilitat, only eight or nine were accepted, and every one had come back to Koolau. I admitted that was true, but it didn't mean the *next* eight or nine wouldn't make it. His comment also said something about how easy life at Koolau was. In time, the controversy died, along with my hopes to do anything constructive at Koolau.

There was no early death for an ongoing fight at Hab II, however. The state Department of Health was now demanding that I give the hospital building back. In fact, they had been asking for a while, and I was still refusing.

The head of the department at that time was George Yuen, who was head of the state sewer department before taking that job. We used to fight a lot, and right in front of his people I said, "George, you keep fucking with us, I will be the biggest thorn in your ass. You will rue the day you ever met or heard the name Vinny Marino or Habilitat. Your people are idiots. They don't know what they're doing. And as a result, they're causing us more confusion than they're giving us help."

I told George if he kept up the harrassment, I'd have two hundred people camping out on his doorstep with a permit, chanting, for two weeks at a time, shitting on his lawn. No way was I going to do this, but according to Machiavellian theories, it's not so important what you do; it's what people *think* you might do that counts.

Pretty soon, I figured a way to keep them more or less off my back. Whenever I got a call from them, I interrupted before they could get into their spiel. I immediately thanked them for calling and asked them for another building, explaining that we were running out of room. For a while my ruse kept them so confused that they didn't insist on our returning their building to them.

After they caught on to what I was doing, though, I had to change my tactics. So when I was told someone was calling from the state hospital, I would have my secretary say I was unavailable, I was in an encounter session or off the facility, and I'd have to call back. Which, of course, I did. However, I would return the call at either 4:05 P.M., five minutes after state quitting time, or at 12:05 P.M., five minutes into the lunch hour. Naturally, no one was there, and I would leave a message because I could always count on the state hospital offices being empty by then, except for the switchboard operator, of course.

Finally, a doctor by the name of Dennis MeeLee, the head of mental health, came to my office and told me that if I didn't return the building to the state hospital, he would hold up our federal funding.

I looked him square in the eye and said, "Dennis, don't be a putz. How are you going to withhold federal money earmarked for Habilitat because of a hassle over a building owned by the state of Hawaii?"

He answered, "Well, that's what I'm going to do," and I replied, "Okay, I'll see you in court."

Which I did, and we beat the bums again. As a matter of fact, every time we had to take them to court to get relief we won. In this case, we got our money, and we also kept the building.

Actually, the rift between Habilitat and the mental health establishment in Hawaii went a lot deeper than a disagreement over a crummy building in Kaneohe. The truth is, they felt *threatened.* What we and other therapeutic communities like ours on the mainland were doing went against just about everything the mental health establishment believed in.

This was a subject I was getting to be an expert about. In the summer of 1977, as the Department of Health in Hawaii started writing a new book of rules for live-in health programs like ours, I was asked to make the keynote speech in Montreal at the Second World Conference of Therapeutic Communities.

By 1977, hundreds of therapeutic communities, or TC's existed—mostly in North America. According to the establishment, we were "the illegitimate child of the mental health movement." I disagreed.

I stood up in front of the crowd of TC directors, psychologists, psychiatrists, and therapists and said, "If the TC can be called a bastard, what shall we call mental health, which has literally squandered billions of dollars working with dope fiends prior to the TC movement? The TC is nobody's bastard. It is a legitimate response to a real need, created by ex-addicts who channeled their energies and intelligence to meet their problems by changing self-destructive and socially disruptive behavior. Since the degreed and credentialed experts couldn't help them change, they had to do it themselves, using unconventional methods and techniques. I am living proof that what we do works."

I said that our success had the so-called professionals worried because we were coming in off the streets—a bunch of thieving ex-cons with no education—and learning in two or three years what twenty years of school hadn't taught them. As a result, they now wanted to control us by passing laws to regulate what we do and how we do it.

Some of these professionals said we were being cruel when we shaved heads, put someone "in the dishpan," or held "brutal" encounter sessions. But what about *their* methods I asked?

"First, the professionals tranquilized their treatment populations so that no one would hurt themselves. Then came electroshock therapy and insulin shock treatments. The real biggy was, of course, the frontal lobotomy, where people were reduced to vegetable states. I've always wondered why they didn't do a rear lobotomy—otherwise known as a rectal."

I wasn't any easier on some of my peers in the audience. It was obvious to me that some people in the TC movement had swallowed the establishment hook. Now *they* were running around in three-piece suits and using all of that intellectual gobbledygook, which we called psychobabble.

I asked if somebody came up and started talking about "differential opportunity structures, inadequate socialization, viable psychosocial communication systems, and the pathology of schismogenetic patterning," would you know what the hell they were talking about?

I told my convention audience, "Some of my peers are actually running around town proud of the title 'paraprofessional.' To me, these people should be labeled 'certified assholes.' It's one thing to be certified to be eligible for funding; it's perverse to be proud of such a title.

"Let's stop using the professional conventions and words. They aren't ours. What are ex-dope fiends doing masquerading as pseudointellectuals, talking in psychoanalytic terms some of us can't even spell, much less pronounce correctly or understand?

"The ex-dope fiend wants to parade around in a conservative three-piece suit and tie while the psychiatrists go the other way and wear groovy tie-dyed dungarees and talk hip to prove they're deep, real human beings. Ex-dope fiends are not psychiatrists and should not act that way unless they, too, want to spend the time in classrooms earning their degrees. Nor will the professional ever be able to equal our cunning, our ability to manipulate, our instinct for survival, or our knowledge of what makes the dope fiend tick, unless he, too, lives our experience."

With an attitude like mine, running around the country and the world making speeches while calling prison and hospital officials assholes to their face at home, what happened next should come as no surprise.

Chapter Fifteen

MY HEAD GOES ON THE CHOPPING BLOCK

I imagine politics in the state of Hawaii are not too different from politics in any other state—I'm just more in touch with and more aware of political affairs here. But I've never understood why anyone would want to go into politics in the first place. We do have one practice in Hawaii that I think is unique. When someone decides to run for election, he or she gathers up all the family and friends, supplies them with garish signs bearing the politician's name and the job he or she is running for, and then the whole group picks a spot by the side of a busy highway.

They stand there for hours every day, rain or shine, and wave their signs and call to the people in the passing cars. I've never understood the thinking behind this approach. I can't believe many people vote for a politician just because they saw him or her and some cousins, or a granddad waving from the side of the road. And I'd be willing to bet that more than one fender-bender resulted when some driver was distracted by waving candidates while barreling along in busy traffic.

One year I got fed up with these wildly gesticulating gatherings on the highway so we dressed one of the residents up as a political candidate, complete with straw hat and sash, gave him a support group of seven or eight other people, and sent them out to stand on a busy corner and wave and call to the passing cars.

The signs they carried said: "Hello—I'm Nobody, Running for Nothing—So Don't Vote for Me."

We did this for four or five days on various corners. The kids got lots of return waves and smiles, and we got a lot of media attention as we moved to different areas of the island.

Another stunt got us similar publicity. We constructed a realistic jail cell, using exact specifications obtained from San Quentin, right down to the bunks, toilet, sink, and aluminum mirror. We dressed three residents up in hustled prison suits and a ball and chain made from papier-mache and put them in the cell on the back of a flatbed truck. On all four sides were signs that read, "Build better people, not better prisons."

For an entire week, the truck was driven around town— to the Hilton Hawaiian Village and along Kalakaua Avenue to the Kahala Hilton Hotel, then into downtown Honolulu by the circuit court right next to the King Kamehameha statue and out to Oahu Prison. Nowhere on the truck or cell was there any mention of Habilitat, and I told my troops if they were asked, only to say, "We're doing this for a good cause."

The media went wild. They followed the truck all week, running pictures in the paper and putting film of the truck on TV. Of course they figured out it was Habilitat, and naturally when they asked, I didn't deny it. We were trying to make a

Residents campaigning on the side of the road.

Vinnie posing in the portable jail cell.

point, and we knew by now that using humor was one of the best ways to do that.

Before long, I found myself embroiled in a much more serious confrontation with local politicians. Part of what made this confrontation unique was the man behind it. Back when Habilitat was surviving on peanut-butter sandwiches, State Senator Duke Kawasaki surprised us with a $25,000 legislative grant. At the time, as I said, I thanked him in a letter, and although we'd never met, I always thought of him in a nice way.

Then, on March 15, 1978, out of a tropical blue sky, Duke Kawasaki and twenty-two others in the state senate called for a full-scale investigation of Habilitat's financial operations. In a memo to Governor Ariyoshi, they said I was recruiting people from the mainland who were putting a strain on local welfare rolls.

The surprising thing about this was that he stood up on the senate floor and publicly demanded the audit when all he needed to do was call the legislative auditor's office and request it. Of course, such a simple act wouldn't have attracted any media attention.

I didn't realize it then, but I have since been advised by a local investigative reporter named Larry Price—who does his homework—that I am what is known as a politician's dream. By this, Larry meant that because of my aggressive personality and the way I constantly stirred up controversy, any politician could assure himself of front-page newspaper coverage, and extensive radio and TV attention, just by mentioning my name. He was right—the next day we were the subject of the lead story for both local newspapers, and we got lots of electronic media attention as well.

We were informed that along with the legislative audit there also would be an Internal Revenue Service audit and a food stamp audit. That meant we were now dealing with both the state of Hawaii and the federal government.

And as if that wasn't enough, I also got word that Governor Ariyoshi was withdrawing my name to serve another term on his Advisory Commission on Drug Abuse and Controlled Substances. (A job I had filled voluntarily and without pay.)

The press told me that earlier that week, at Kawasaki's request, Andy Chang, head of the DSSH, supplied a list showing seventy percent of our residents who were on welfare were from outside Hawaii. And that, according to Chang, made it look like we were recruiting on the mainland.

At first I tried to be calm and rational. I said the charge about our stuffing the welfare rolls with mainlanders was ridiculous. Habilitat received federal money, and we couldn't legally discriminate against out-of-staters any more than we could discriminate for racial or sexual reasons. If, after these people were in Hawaii, they qualified for welfare, I couldn't do anything about that either.

I said, "Ever since we've gotten national exposure, we have people coming in here from around the world. To me it doesn't matter where these people come from because they're human beings. If a guy comes in here and needs help, we don't turn him away. I can't be responsible for where they come from."

The reporters presented figures provided by Chang, who said the DSSH was paying Habilitat more than $731,000 a year in welfare, rent deposits, and counseling services. He also said the Department of Health was paying Habilitat about $363,000 for drug abuse programs, part of that from federal funds.

To which I said, "So what?" If we qualified for state and federal help, we deserved it. It only provided a third of our budget anyway. The other two-thirds came from fees charged to families of residents, private contributions, and our fund-raising and business activities.

As for the audit itself, I said Habilitat was privately audited every year in compliance with state and federal requirements. We also sent a yearly financial report to DSSH, which was probably where Andy Chang got his figures.

"By the way," I said, "I don't think it's a coincidence that Kawasaki launched this investigation three days after our telethon. We got $313,000 in pledges, and how much do you think we'll collect now that everybody and his goddamned cousin is on our case?

"If Kawasaki was really interested in Habilitat, he could've come here any time. But he hasn't crossed our doorstep once over the seven years we've been here."

Somebody asked me what I thought of Kawasaki, personally.

I said, "The man is a moron and an idiot."

Immediately, it seemed as though almost everybody in the state government jumped on me. Andy Chang attacked Habilitat again, and so did Beadie Dawson, a state public relations spokeswoman.

I remember calling Ms. Dawson a "dizzy broad," and I remember telling Andy that he should spend more time running the prison and the welfare system and get off my back.

Then came the Department of Health, and I told them, "Go learn how to run your state hospital before coming to me with criticism of my efforts, especially since nobody in state government really has any knowledge about Habilitat and what it is accomplishing."

Next morning, Habilitat was again the subject of the *Honolulu Advertiser's* lead story. My friend Aku did his damnedest to defend me and to attack Duke Kawasaki and Andy Chang on his popular early morning radio show. All the local TV stations carried the story too. Knowing I had nothing to worry about, I really didn't care, and my troops were excited about the whole affair. It pleased them to realize I could cause such a noise throughout the state. It didn't, however, please anyone at Habilitat when, as we feared, the collection of telethon pledges fell to sixty percent.

Then just as evidence of the negative impact from the threatened audit was revealing itself, the legislature shelved the whole idea. After all that furor, the issue of an audit was dead.

I couldn't believe it. Was this man trying to make me crazy? Right away, I wrote a letter to people who made pledges but who hadn't sent their money yet. I said the audit had been canceled: "The legislature confirmed that they do in fact have all the information after all. Having made headlines and captured attention, the issue is no longer useful as a legitimate probe nor to gain any more headlines."

I thought that was that, but no. The day after we mailed the letter, the legislature changed its mind *again* and ordered the audit after all. And Duke Kawasaki went to the press with a copy of the letter I had mailed and called me a liar.

This man *was* making me crazy!

I still had the skull that I took from our resident warlock. One day when I put out a cigarette in it, my brother Frank spoke up. "Vinny, I'm telling you, that skull is hard luck, you ought to get rid of it."

I said, "You mean Oscar? Oscar's been on my desk for a long time. I can't get rid of Oscar."

"I'm telling you, it's not natural to have a skull. You got to take it and throw the fucking thing in the ocean as far as you can."

"Frank, you been telling me this for years. I'm not superstitious."

Frank just shrugged, and I picked up the skull and looked at it. I said, "I don't know, maybe it *is* the fucking skull."

So I took it from my office, and I went out to the beach and threw it into Kaneohe Bay. Then I went home.

That night, I was in bed with my wife, and the news came on. The lead story was about a skull that had been found on the beach in Kaneohe. Police were investigating the possibility of a homicide. We started laughing, and the phone rang. It was Dudley Hoolhurst, my controller, and she was hysterical.

She said, "Vinny, they found Oscar!"

So I had to call the police and say, "This is Vinny Marino at Habilitat. You know that skull you found?"

By the time I finished telling my story, there was a long silence at the other end of the phone.

I said, "Honest, officer."

Now it was the cop's turn to be hysterical—with laughter.

The audit took almost eight months to complete. By law, we were supposed to receive a copy and have a chance to respond before any information was released to the media.

You can imagine my astonishment when I got a phone call in my office one evening from a local newspaper reporter, who told me he had in his possession a copy of the audit and the allegations the state was making against us. He asked if I wanted to make any comments. We had only received our copy of the state's allegations against us a few hours before and were just beginning to prepare our response to all the bullshit they had come up with.

I asked him politely how he had managed to get a copy of such a confidential document, and he answered, "Look, I have my own sources. Do you want to make a comment?"

I remember telling him whatever his source was, it was illegal for him to have this copy, that the report should not have been made public before my board of directors and I had an opportunity to respond.

Again, he asked, "Do you want to make a comment?" I hung up without answering.

The next day all hell broke loose. We again made the front page of both newspapers, and we were the lead story for all the local TV and radio stations. The night before, I had carefully gone over every word of the audit report, and I couldn't believe the kind of bullshit the auditors had come up with.

First, they accused me of nepotism since my brother Frank, my wife Vickie, and my daughter Lila were all employees of Habilitat. The state wanted to know how much money the Marino family made.

In response, I pointed out that Vickie had been a resident first, then an employee of Habilitat even before we were married, and that Lila had spent three-and-a-half years as a resident of Habilitat. She had never even smoked a cigarette, much less used any drugs, including alcohol. She just had what might be termed a behavioral disorder—in essence, she was spoiled. After she graduated the program, she was hired to work for Habilitat as many of our graduates are.

My brother had come to Hawaii at my request to help me set up Habilitat's sales and marketing division as one of our vocational training entities. He had expertise in this field since for many years he had operated his own sales company, and he was in complete agreement with my feelings about job training being vitally important to the complete rehabilitation of our residents.

As for how much we made, I told the press it was none of their business, but if they wanted to look it up, it was a matter of public record. (I was making $39,000 a year at the time.)

The state's second charge involved the house my family and I were living in. In 1974, Jerry Greenspan—as an incentive to persuade me to remain at Habilitat for at least three years—

came up with the idea that Habilitat would purchase a house in Kailua where my family and I could live. Vickie and I would make the mortgage payments, and if I was still around in 1977, I would be allowed to refinance the house with a mortgage in my own name at the price the house had been bought for in 1974. The deal also included an agreement that during these three years from 1974 to 1977, I would receive no increases in my salary.

It sounded good to me, and it also sounded good to Evan Shirley, who was the corporate attorney for Habilitat. I brought the subject up at a board meeting. At that time, the board included five other attorneys in addition to Evan Shirley. Fred Titcomb, then president of the board and an attorney, signed the motion, which was made and seconded, to the effect that the above-mentioned house deal was okay. I figured with the approval of six attorneys, I had to be safe.

We lived in the house from 1974 until 1977, at which time I exercised my option to buy the house from Habilitat.

As it happened, we had just acquired a new corporate attorney, an intelligent and conservative man named Ed Bendet. In an effort to familiarize himself with our organization, he began to review the minutes of all Habilitat's board meetings from the time of its inception.

When he came to the house deal, he was horrified. He told me the agreement was completely illegal and should never have been considered, let alone consummated. We called an emergency board meeting to discuss the situation, and at this meeting a motion was presented and carried that I should return the house to Habilitat.

Please bear in mind I had just closed a deal two weeks earlier with State Savings and Loan, which gave me a mortgage to purchase the house. Can you imagine the feelings of the poor guy I had dealt with there when I went back to him and told him I had to sell it back to Habilitat? He must have thought I was crazy.

My board of directors hired three separate appraisers to evaluate the property, and I sold it back to Habilitat for the lowest appraisal. Incidentally, that house, purchased for $90,000, sold in 1985 for $202,000. I ended up with no house, no raises for the three-year period, and got the shit kicked out of me in every newspaper and on every radio and TV station in the state. Such is life!

I could have chosen to sue Evan Shirley and the other attorneys on the board for malpractice since they should have known better, but I believed they were well-intentioned men who had made a mistake. I took it on the jaw and rolled with the punch.

Of course, my feelings were really hurt, and I felt my image had been badly damaged, but the thing that upset me the most was that no one on my board of directors came forward to exonerate me and publicly admit responsibility for the mistake. I was a completely innocent victim, and I explained this to the legislative auditors in answer to their indictment. They did not want to see it, hear it, or believe it, however.

Their third allegation was that my board of directors was a "rubber stamp" board and that, in actuality, I ran Habilitat without any kind of legal governing body. I replied that this accusation was completely false, that my board—as with most boards serving nonprofit organizations—concerned itself largely with fiduciary responsibilities. They carefully checked our monthly financial statements and our annual audit report. They followed up on my stated goals to assure that I was accomplishing them. After a very deliberate study of programs and institutions similar to ours, they set my salary and Vickie's. They also determined my brother Frank's salary. What more could be expected of a board of directors?

It became only too obvious that the state of Hawaii was out to discredit me and Habilitat, probably because of the stands I had taken against various politicians, the prison system, the state hospital, and the morons who run these institutions. I must have gotten at least thirty calls from various reporters all over the state. As distraught as I was, one funny incident came out of it. Several months earlier, Vickie and I had been watching TV one evening, and someone—I don't remember who—was being pestered by reporters, and he kept saying, "No comment, no comment," in answer to whatever they asked.

At the time, I said to Vickie, "One of these days I would love to be able to do that."

She just laughed and answered, "You could never do that."

Now my chance had come, and I got a lot of satisfaction out of repeating, "No comment" to all the reporters' questions. They had expected my usual vitriolic explosion and were dumbfounded when they couldn't lure me into any kind of discussion.

Normally, my response would have ended any further media interest in this area, but the next day, on Saturday morning, while I was driving to work, I passed a newsboy on a street corner. He held up his papers and across the front page, in huge red letters, I read, "HABILITAT'S LICENSE BEING PULLED." Even in my anger and despair, I had to chuckle. Habilitat never had a license.

Now it was really apparent the state had declared war, and for the next thirteen days and nights, my key staff, myself, and a man named Dennis Clark, who had offered his help, ripped the state's charges to shreds. We studied each attack and allegation separately, then stamped each one with a large black-inked "Bullshit—False Report." (This was a rubber stamp I kept in my desk to use on many government forms and correspondence.) Then we carefully explained the truth about the subject and upon completion, returned the corrected copy to the auditor's office.

My board of directors were hurt and unhappy about the unsupported charges and implications in the audit. They were cautious and civilized people, however, and most of them took the attitude that our best approach would be to murmur some apologies in defense of the audit and try to make peace with the state.

My board president at that time was an extremely intelligent and charming lady named Karen White. As a probation officer for the state's family court system, which works with juveniles, she had a lot of experience in dealing with bureaucracy in its many forms. Over the years she'd tried hard to get me to change some of my aggressive mannerisms and clean up my language. She, in particular, was insistent that I back down and soften my response. But this time I couldn't go along with her wishes. I was tired of defending—it went against what I believed.

I explained to the board that in the school of hard knocks where I got my degree I was taught that (1) you never defend, (2) you always attack, (3) you never attack on your own turf, (4) you always attack on their turf, and (5) you always take more out of them than they take out of you. This was the attitude with which I went into the news conference I called.

On the way to the news conference, which I had called at Hab II, I noticed the driver was nervously chain-smoking and sweating profusely. I asked him to pull over to the side of the road, and I calmed him down, telling him not to worry. I waited right there until I knew everyone else would be at the meeting. Then I asked him to take me to the side entrance so that when I entered the TV lights and cameras would come on, and I could get right into it without being diverted by board members I knew were waiting to make a final pitch for love, peace, and harmony.

The plan worked beautifully. As soon as I stepped up to the podium, I opened fire. I charged the DSSH with gross incompetency; I attacked the Department of Health for its operation of the state hospital; and I called the people who ran the state prison system a bunch of idiots. I tore into them with all the rage that had been festering in me for two long weeks.

While I was delivering my opinions, one of the local TV reporters kept waving a piece of paper at me, but I was too wound up to pay any attention. Finally, Vickie came up and whispered to me, "Vinny, listen to what this man has to say. He's on our side."

I turned back to the reporter, and he handed me a paper from the U.S. Food and Drug Administration, angrily denouncing the DSSH and accusing them of gross negligence for not having been on Habilitat's property for almost three years.

When the press conference broke up, my board members were in a state of shock, but I repeated to them we had no reason to apologize. We were a reputable organization, and the state of Hawaii had not only been unfair and abusive to us, they had also been negligent in their own duties. Then I gathered Vickie and our daughter Victoria, and we went home.

Later we turned on the TV to find out what approach the media would take. We were amazed to find that on every station, the tide had turned. We now had all the media staunchly supporting us.

Tears ran down my cheeks, and when I looked at Vickie, she was crying, too. Little Victoria, who was four, was frightened by our tears, and she began to cry. I took her in my arms and said, "Don't be upset, Sweetheart—these are good tears. We won! We beat the rats!"

Chapter Sixteen

TAKING CARE OF BUSINESS

T his didn't mean we were out of the line of fire entirely, but for a while the heat cooled slightly. In fact, we were starting to receive some praise. A lot of it was coming from the mainland. The first came in a story Steve Allen wrote for the *Los Angeles Times*. Steve had been one of Synanon's early supporters. Now, twenty years later, in an article about drug rehabilitation centers, he said Habilitat was one of the best.

My "friend" from the *New York Post*, columnist James Wechsler, chimed in. "This is a time when the word 'rehabilitation' is in wide disrepute," he wrote, "consigned by the tough-minded to the vocabulary of obsolete sentimentalities. But those who have refused to concede the debate is over should find sustenance in the story of Vincent Marino's remarkable journey from the depths."

Wechsler had written about me when I was in New York and mistakenly identified in a brutal assault and robbery case. When I beat the rap, he devoted two columns to me, and now, eight years later, I had decided to bring him up to date so I wrote him about Habilitat.

"It has been a rough pilgrimage from New York's 'Little Italy' for Vincent Marino, who once awakened from a heroin binge to find a 'dead-on-arrival' tag tied to his big toe and who had last rites administered to him on too many occasions and so narrowly evaded a long-term sentence in 1970. By every current standard of rage, he might have been easily branded socially incurable. Now—and for over eight years—he has been rescuing and rehabilitating others. Mission impossible?"

Only three weeks after that appeared, more praise came from right here in Hawaii when Frank Fasi delivered a seminar for my troops. His son, Carl, was facing forgery and burglary charges and had gone to court that week. Carl had a long history of drug use and was being held in jail. Frank refused to bail him out. Frank believed in the concept of "tough love," which says you have to take away the safety net and let the individual in trouble hit bottom before you can expect any change.

Frank stood in front of my troops and with a shaking voice, he told them, "I only wish my son were sitting here tonight among you."

We also got praise from drug rehabilitation professionals who came to Hawaii, people like Frank Natale who, once they were in the islands, gave interviews in which they flattered us. Frank wasn't the only expert to come out. John Mahar was another. He was the founder and director of a program in San Francisco called Delancey Street, and he flew in a month after

Duke Kawasaki released the audit report. John called the report an "excellent professional hatchet job."

Another time I called in Dr. Frederick B. Glaser, head of psychiatry at Toronto's Addiction Research Foundation, to evaluate the program. I told the press—and this was true—that I couldn't be all that objective. I needed someone from the outside to take a good, hard look and make some recommendations if they seemed to be needed. Glaser spent four days with me and my staff, looking us over. When he was interviewed by the Honolulu media, he said Habilitat compared very favorably with other drug treatment communities and in some respects "is in the forefront."

We were getting other visitors to Habilitat in 1978, 1979, and 1980, and their presence helped us, too. These were the first national celebrities. Local celebrities had supported us all along—attending our luaus and graduations, performing at our concerts and telethons, contributing recipes to our cookbooks. We valued these friends tremendously, but I believed national stars would ultimately be the ones to put us on the map. The first to visit, in May 1978, was Shaun Cassidy, the singer and star of "The Hardy Boys" television show. He was appearing at Honolulu's International Center, and often visited hospitals while touring. When his promoter suggested he check out Habilitat, Shaun agreed. He told me that his promoter had said, "It's a bit different from anything else you've seen, but I think you'll like it."

Shaun told me that he had been reluctant, but once he was on the facility and talking with the troops he "got into it real quick." He told me and the residents that when he was fifteen and sixteen and going to boarding school after growing up spoiled in Beverly Hills—the son of two famous movie stars (Shirley Jones and Jack Cassidy)—he had problems, too. And after listening to some of the residents tell their stories, he realized that their problems weren't all that different from his own.

David Braun said, "The problems are universal, and it doesn't have all that much to do with drugs."

Before the year was out, the former heavyweight champion of the world, Joe Frazier, visited us, and in 1980, Bob Newhart and Don Rickles came. Newhart and Rickles heard about us from Danny Kaleikini, a local singer, when they met at the Kahala Hilton, a popular Honolulu hotel for the Hollywood set where Danny performs. They were scheduled to play golf together the afternoon that Newhart and Rickles came out to Habilitat, but these two gentlemen were so impressed by what they saw and heard, they stayed all day and blew their golf game.

On the way back to California, the Newharts met someone on the plane who gave them a cockamamie story about being related to the owner of a well-known vineyard or brewery. This guy had a drug problem, and because of just meeting me and touring Habilitat, Bob and Ginnie Newhart took him home with them. Bob phoned me and said he wanted to know what to do.

I said, "First thing is you get that guy out of your house. You've got your family to think of. You've got valuables in the house. You don't need this, Bob. Get rid of him and give him Habilitat's number, tell him to call me."

Bob said he felt a bit foolish. I told him that he was just being a nice guy, but he really did have to be more careful. He replied that he was ignorant about drugs.

We talked for a while, and before we were finished, he asked me if I'd come to Los Angeles to conduct a seminar in his home. I suggested that he and Ginnie and the Rickles put the word out to see if they could get any interest going. Then we'd talk again.

I'd been conducting seminars in Hawaii since 1978, when I teamed up with Dr. Judianne Densen-Gerber of Odyssey House to do a workshop in family survival techniques called, "Is the Family Unit an Endangered Species?" Odyssey House was one of the country's better-known rehabilitation centers, and Judy and I had been sharing experiences for many years. We also shared a concern about what was happening to the family. The way we saw it, more and more parents were screwing up, and their kids were going on the rocks because of it.

Though my mother always told me children were borrowed, most people in this country believe they *own* their children. This is wrong headed and dangerous. Parents don't own their kids; they owe them. They have a responsibility to them. The truth is, the kids should have all the rights.

Many years ago, a child was born into a larger family or community situation. The church congregation greeted the new child. The village rejoiced at the new child. Each child was part of an extended family, what is called 'ohana in Hawaii.

This concept influenced every aspect of Hawaiian life. When a family didn't have enough to eat, others shared what food they had. No one went without. It was a loving, caring community—a big family. This is what Habilitat was—in fact, had been since it started. We took in the "strays," the same way ancient Hawaiians did, and gave them love and nurturing. Unfortunately, this is not always the way it is in the world.

Kids today are born into isolation. They experience constant uprooting and an absence of grandparents, aunts and uncles and cousins. More and more parents are abusing their kids—psychologically, physically, emotionally, and at times sexually. At the same time, parents are compromising themselves with drugs and other problems. They are becoming poor role models, and not surprisingly the kids are mimicking them.

A lot of the people who came to Habilitat as teenagers are second-generation drug and alcohol abusers. It was an ugly, awful merry-go-round in some families.

The response to our seminars in Hawaii was miserable. We advertised in the papers. We put up posters, distributed flyers, and got publicity in all the local papers, and the people did *not* come out. All I could do was hope that in California the reaction would be more promising.

The Newharts and Rickles sent 250 flyers to friends and acquaintances and scheduled the seminar in a large dining room of the Bel-Air Hotel. When I arrived with Richie Rivera, who was handling Habilitat's publicity, Ginnie greeted me with a long face.

She said, "We only have about fifty acceptances, which means we might have a hundred. I think that's terrifying. The feedback I'm getting is that a lot of parents don't want to show up at a thing like this. They're afraid people will think their kids are on drugs. And then some of the parents I talk to say, 'Well, these are very socially acceptable drugs.' They're talking about everything from grass to coke to Quaaludes. What're we going to do?"

I told her we'd have the seminar. Now she was beginning to understand the uphill fight we all faced.

Bob couldn't help opening with a little joke, saying, "I don't know anyone here who hasn't been touched by this problem. In their own family, their friends, through robberies and burglaries."

That was the end of the humor. The subject of the seminar, drug abuse and what it does to families, was no laughing matter. Bob was the first to admit it. He said he was naive and wouldn't know how to spot the signs of drug abuse if they showed up in his children. (Rob was then sixteen, Timothy thirteen.) And that was part of why he felt he had to sponsor the seminar. A lot of people needed education on the subject, just like he did.

Others in Hollywood were not so innocent. Carol Burnett had recently revealed that one of her children was having serious problems with drugs. The night before the seminar, about a twenty-minute drive from the Bel-Air Hotel, Richard Pryor had set himself on fire while allegedly freebasing cocaine. Because of this, we got a lot of space in the media including pictures of me, Richie, Bob, Don, and another big star who came, Carroll O'Connor.

When people like Shaun Cassidy, Joe Frazier, Bob Newhart, Don Rickles, Carroll O'Connor, and others visited Habilitat or attended Habilitat-sponsored events, it worked for us in several ways. The visits were a real boost for the residents. It made them feel good that well-known people cared enough to take time from their busy schedules to visit.

Whenever national stars got involved with us, it also gave Habilitat broader recognition and credibility. Naturally, we reprinted the stories with the pictures of the celebrities and included them with our publicity mailings. We used the association to bring more attention to Habilitat. And with the attention came more money.

In June 1979, Habilitat made national headlines on its own, not because of these celebrities. This time the publicity was because of a resident. The story started two years before when I got a phone call from a guy who told me his name was Joe Cascone, calling from New York. He said he wanted to come out.

I said, "You're from New York. There're lots of programs between there, the West Coast, and us. Why Hawaii?"

He told me he heard about me, and if I could make it, he felt like he had a shot. He said he was thirty-five years old, had spent nineteen years in prison in places like Greenhaven,

Sing Sing, and Attica, and every time he came out he immediately went back to using drugs—that's all he knew.

Joe said, "I'm tired of chasing a cooker. I'm tired of sticking needles in my arm. Life's passing me by. One more
chance, that's all I need, to see if I can make it clean."

He seemed to have the right kind of attitude for what
we consider an old-time dope fiend who's run the gamut and
is really tired of the same old trips. People his age usually
realize that one of two things will happen to them—either
they will die or they will spend the rest of their lives in
prison.

I told Joe to get on a plane and be sure to bring all his ID
along. We'd meet him at the airport and give him an interview.
That's all we promised. If he seemed sincere, he was in. If not,
we would send him back to New York—Hawaii already had too
many dope fiends.

We set the interview up, and no matter how rough we all
got with him, it didn't matter. We called him all kinds of
names, and after a half hour of that, I said, "Joe, you're sitting
here getting abused—what's happening with you? What are
you feeling?"

"I've been abused all my life, but the feeling I got now is
this is the last time, and this time it's for a different reason."

One of the residents present said, "Okay, what is it you
want?"

"I need help."

"I can't hear you, punk."

Joe yelled louder. From the other side of the room someone else said, "What are you, a sissy, is that the loudest you can
yell?"

All of a sudden, from the bottom of some goddamned pit
somewhere in hell came the most awful scream I'd ever heard.
When it stopped, Joe was crying like a baby.

Finally I cut him short and said, "Okay, Joe, you got it. Welcome to Habilitat."

Joe was born and raised in Brooklyn, and he had the thickest, gruffest Damon Runyan accent that I ever heard outside of watching an old movie. Physically, like a lot of guys who had done big time, he was muscular from all the weight-lifting that so many convicts use to fill their days.

No matter how hard Joe tried, though, he couldn't do anything right. He'd go forward two steps, then back three. Despite his many screwups, Joe eventually made it to reentry and was assigned to the landscaping crew. He'd been in the program for sixteen months when I got a call from a Honolulu police detective I knew named Tony. Tony said one of the people in the program was wanted in Duchess County, state of New York, for escape from a hospital for the criminally insane.

"Yeah," I said, "What's his name?"

"Poveromo. Louis Poveromo."

"Nobody here by that name."

The detective said, "He also goes by Joe Cascone."

"Oh-oh. I think we got a problem."

Turns out Cascone-Poveromo had entered Habilitat with a figazy ID after escaping from Matteawan State Prison for the Criminally Insane, where he was serving a ten-to-twenty year term for armed robbery. He'd been one of ten convicts in the escape—the largest in New York history—and the only one never caught.

I told the detective I'd call him right back. Then I had Joe brought to my office. He admitted he was Poveromo.

"What do you want to do?" I said.

"Run. I want to run."

I said that was okay with me, but if he ran, he was on his own. If he stayed and turned himself in, I said I'd stick with him, and I'd do everything I could to keep him in Habilitat. He thought it over for a minute and said he'd take a shot with me. I explained I could offer no guarantee, but I would go all out to help him.

Next I called Dave Schutter to handle the legal end. Then I called the detective and said we were bringing him in. The detective said "Vinny, the telex calls him extremely dangerous, repeat, extremely dangerous."

I said, "Take a look at my rap sheet, I was extremely dangerous too. We have a lot of people at Habilitat who used to be extremely dangerous."

We gave him a carton of cigarettes and some money, knowing they'd throw him back into jail. The next day, Dave and I went to court, and the local judge allowed him to return to Habilitat in my custody.

Another eight months went by before Dave Schutter—who, by the way, handled the case without charge—exhausted all the avenues of extradition. Finally, in June 1979, the local court said he had to go back to New York. I asked the judge if I could take him back personally rather than send him in shackles with a police escort. To my mind the man had changed in two years, and I thought he deserved that much respect. The judge granted my request. That night I told my guys to take "Joe" out, find a good, clean hooker, and get him laid.

Then I took up a collection from staff members, Habilitat's Board of Directors, parents of some of the residents, as well as myself, and we formed the Louis Poveromo Fund to offset the cost of our airfare to New York as well as pay for a New York public relations firm and a New York attorney, both of whom were to meet us at the airport. We arrived with a splash because I wanted to tell the story of Joe's rehabilitation. Although I didn't really have much hope, I hadn't quite given up saving him from jail.

On June 14 we arrived at John F. Kennedy Airport,

greeted by ten or twelve reporters. The next day we were head-line news. Unfortunately, it wasn't enough to turn the tide, and Joe was returned to jail. He did, however, beat one of the out-standing charges against him—the one for escaping from the mental hospital. They dropped that because if you're suppos-edly insane, how can you be held accountable? In my opinion, the lawyer didn't do as well as I thought he could've. Too bad Dave Schutter wasn't there with us.

While I was in New York, naturally I went to see my mom and dad. It was the last time I saw my mom alive.

Four months later, back in Hawaii, I got a call from my friend Dick Jensen. Dick had performed at most of our benefits, and he wanted me to have dinner with him and Glen Larson, a Hollywood producer who was interested in making a movie based on my life. I accepted this invitation, and on October 21, 1979, Vickie and I drove to the Ala Moana Ameri-cana Hotel for what I thought would be a quiet dinner. As I opened the door to the dining room, the lights went on and hundreds of people stood up and cheered. It was a testimonial dinner organized by Vickie, my brother Frank, and Frank Cockett. Mayor Fasi gave me a plaque for being the "Out-standing Citizen of the Seventies." I couldn't believe it! Me, a guy who always figured he knew everything that was going on. I was completely surprised.

There were in-person testimonials from Ethel Azama, whose two kids had gotten involved with Habilitat, from Aku, Dick Jensen, the mayor, and many others. Frank Cockett also made a moving speech.

Letters came from Senator Ted Kennedy, Steve Allen and Jayne Meadows, Pearl Bailey, George Burns, Jean Stapleton, and Bill Cosby. There was even a message from Pope Paul, who sent a special apostolic blessing as a pledge of divine grace and favor.

Finally Aku, who was MCing the dinner, called me up. The tune "My Way" was being played on the piano. It was a song that Aku had dedicated to me many times on his radio show during the period when Habilitat was being audited.

By now I had nearly a dozen leis around my neck and felt like the racehorse Man-o'War. I was still in shock. Finally I cleared my throat and said, "Usually the thank-yous I get are seeing people I have helped. They don't even have to say thank you. I see people like me who have been reunited with their families after going to the very bottom. Today, seeing people change is my shot of dope. I'm not saying we've got the panacea for the world's ills, but we do have one damn good answer for some people."

I was getting really choked up, and I was thinking of my mom in New York. I said, "I just wish that my mom could've been here." I couldn't say any more so I sat down.

Less than forty-eight hours later, my brother Joey called to say my mom had died of cancer. I flew to New York for the funeral. When I returned, I knew that when we finally got our new institutional kitchen, dining room, and dormitories, we'd call it the "Mother Gemma Wing." That's where she always wanted to be—near the kitchen.

Our building finally got under way in May 1980 when First Hawaiian Bank approved a $600,000 loan. Imagine that: Me, a longtime scamming junkie, proven thief, and excon, straight and responsible enough to get a bank to loan us more than half a million dollars!

We hired a local construction company and broke ground in July. That was when I came up with another great fundraising idea, although everyone else thought it was crazy at the time.

A lot of our regular fund-raising sources were drying up. We had decided to stop selling advertising specialties. We

The stages of construction of the Mother Gemma building.

never did make much money at it. That wasn't the only reason
we got into the business, but with travel costs increasing
tremendously, we could soon start losing money—and that we
couldn't afford.

The competition was picking up too. Once, when our
people were trying to open up Minnesota, they found themselves going head-to-head with salespeople from both Synanon
and Delancey Street. All three of us were in the same place at
the same time, a surprise to everyone. We got a good laugh out
of the situation, but it showed how crowded the market was
getting.

When my brother Frank decided to return to New York
with his family—after being able to take pride in knowing his
job was done—I figured it was a good time to sell the business.
He'd been with Habilitat for six years, coordinating the marketing and supervising most of the sales training. When he
left, I sold the Hawaii business to a group of local graduates
who wanted to continue and the rest to a mainland company.

The third *Homegrown* album was also the last. We'd
netted nearly $82,000 on *Homegrown Two*, but the sales push
for *Homegrown Three* included several desperation moves. For
example, "two albums for the price of one, buy *Homegrown
Three* and get *Homegrown Two* for free," and we still only netted $20,000. For us, the recording industry was played out as a
money source.

We also stopped doing telethons. In 1979 we had staged
our fourth, cutting it from fifteen to nine-and-a-half hours and
focusing the attention on education rather than entertainment. The donations were good—we got pledges for $98,000
and eventually collected $107,000—but it was clear to us that
this idea was winding down too. Everybody and his brother
were doing telethons in Hawaii by now. And besides, I had a
new idea.

It came to me as I watched a bulldozer cruise toward one of the brick walls on the property to knock it down and make room for the new building. I hollered for the operator to stop.

I went over to the guy and said, "Don't knock it down. Take it down a brick at a time. We're going to sell those bricks."

Frank Cockett was nearby and he said, "Vinny, let him knock it down. We're only getting twelve cents a brick."

I said, "No, Frank. That's what we were offered. I've decided we're going to sell them for a minimum of twenty-five dollars."

"Each?"

I smiled at the look on his face. "That's right, Frank. We're going to sell them for a minimum of twenty-five dollars, a maximum of a thousand."

Vickie's comment when she heard what I wanted to do was like Frank's response: "I think the old man has finally gone off the deep end."

Of course I had a plan. What we did was wash and dry the bricks, laminate them, then put a felt backing on the bottom, and a brass plate on the opposite side. For a contribution of twenty-five dollars or more, we said we'd engrave the donor's name and any other brief sentiment on the plaque. The donor also got a brief history of the Bigelow estate and a "stock certificate" showing "ownership" of Habilitat.

It wasn't real ownership we were offering—only symbolic ownership—and something tangible a person could place in a position of prominence at home or in the office, showing the owner had an interest in Habilitat. Plus, it was a good conversation piece. How many people do you know who have paid up to a thousand dollars for a fifty-eight-year-old laminated brick?

We actually offered two kinds of stock. On one certificate we played it straight, saying the donor "has made a worthwhile contribution toward the fulfillment of human potential representing but a minute portion of the infinite worth of a human life." This stock share entitled the owner "to partake in the celebration of life and its best values: Love, Hope and Compassion."

The second type of stock certificate was more popular. It entitled the purchaser to "full protection against and exemption from involvement in future audits of Habilitat, waking up in the morning to find Habilitat has moved in next door during the night, Habilitat's picketing your place of business or camping out on your front lawn, or being called a 'moron' by Habilitat's executive director."

Before we were finished with that campaign, we took in $44,000. Not bad for a pile of funky bricks.

It was at this time—after a lot of unnecessary stalling—that the Department of Health gave us a license to operate, the license we never had that the newspapers had said was being revoked. What a joke! I also resigned my position on the Habilitat board. This was in direct response to the state audit, of course.

I have to admit that it did look a little funny to be a member of a board that set my own salary but that never really occurred to me. I also don't think my salary at the time was out of line with the salaries of other people running any organization of Habilitat's size and complexity. We had more than forty staff members and consultants and a hundred and fifty-plus residents, with an annual budget of close to $3 million. I had always abstained from voting on my salary or those of my family too. The day after the board meeting when I resigned, I sent out a press release saying that I hoped this would prove I wasn't running a one-man show, as charged, and that Habilitat was making every effort to follow the recommendations suggested by the state—as silly as they were.

I did however, keep my title as executive director. I also

The wall that turned into a novel fundraiser.

The final product, a brick penholder.

reserved the right to sit in on board meetings as a nonvoting observer.

Besides me, the board also lost Karen White, a member since the early days. Losing Karen was hard. She was still employed by family court, and because we were getting referrals from that court, the state Ethics Commission ruled that her position at Habilitat represented a possible conflict of interest.

When I resigned, we added eight new members to the board, bringing the total to fourteen, the largest it had ever been. One was Russ Francis, who was identified in the press release as president of Executive Air Charters, but he was better known for his professional football career with the New England Patriots and later with the San Francisco Forty-Niners. Russ was a local boy who grew up not far from Habilitat's original home in Kailua, and he had been one of our longtime supporters.

I don't want to give the impression that I was now a perfect angel. I may have been trying the halo on for a fit, but that didn't mean I wore it straight or all the time. Even after Frank Fasi gave me the "Outstanding Citizen of the Seventies" award, I was taking shots at the establishment—because I believed as I always had that a moron is a moron.

In 1980, I was still battling it out with the Department of Health over the buildings on the hospital grounds and still asking to take over Koolau. At this time the state legislature passed a bill giving Andy Chang, director of social services, the right to investigate what we charged the state for housing people. We charged $175 per person for rent and utilities, the maximum allowed by the state, and a piddling sum, I thought. Seventy-five of our people were court referrals, which came to $13,125 a month. Chang thought it was too much, although eventually he let it stand.

I was still taking shots at my peers at conventions, too. Never, ever, did I let up when it came to self-sufficiency. Again and again I warned the other TC's—the day of the handout was coming to an end. In Seattle I also told them I thought they were hypocrites because they drank more booze there than a wine-tasting contest in France consumed. In Boston I said the members of the national association should boycott next year's scheduled meeting in New Orleans because Louisiana had rejected the Equal Rights Amendment. A few years later, when I quit making speeches at TCA conventions, they begged me to come back. They said I stirred things up, that the meetings were boring without me.

But as 1980 came to a close, things were going great. The Alcohol and Drug Abuse branch of the Department of Health gave us a clean bill of health. As a result of my relationship with Don Rickles and Bob Newhart, I got a shot on the Merv Griffin television show. I'd also been working with some writers on my autobiography, and Playboy Productions took an option on the movie rights.

All that was in November of 1980. Two months later I wasn't sure I had a life story to sell. In January 1981, I had a heart attack.

Chapter Seventeen

THE BOTTOM FALLS OUT

Decem ber 3, 1980, was one of the best days of my life. Thanks to my friends Bob Newhart and Don Rickles, I was riding a high better than anything dope had given me. After that seminar at the Bel Air Hotel, a couple of Hollywood producers approached me to do a movie based on my life. I asked Don what I should do, and he turned me over to his manager, Joe Scandori, who got a theatrical attorney to negotiate for me.

At the same time, Don's manager was suggesting to several television talk shows that I'd make a terrific team with Don. It all came together in the green room of the "Merv Griffin Show" in Los Angeles. Then while waiting to go on camera and be interviewed with Don, the attorney brought me a contract from Playboy Productions. *Playboy* magazine had been producing television shows for several years and wanted my story to be a made-for-television feature film. With Vickie at my side, I signed the contract, giving *Playboy* a six-months option on my story. If nothing developed in six months, all rights would return to me.

Just before we went into the studio, Don told me he hoped I wouldn't get upset if he didn't really endorse the Habilitat program wholeheartedly. He said he just didn't do that sort of thing. I wasn't disappointed. I was grateful to have the opportunity to be on national television. Then when we got on camera, Don delivered the most incredible praise I've ever heard.

Boy was I riding a wave of good feelings when Vickie and I returned to Hawaii. Christmas and New Year's were coming up. After that, Don's people had locked in an appearance on the "Mike Douglas Show" for January 19, and a week after that, Habilitat would mark its tenth anniversary. We weren't planning anything unusual, but everyone was pretty excited.

Then, on January 15, while meeting in my office with one of my board members, I felt some pain in my chest and left arm. I asked the head of medical to come to my office, and when I explained what was happening, he got very serious and phoned a doctor in Kailua for an emergency visit. He said he wanted to take me to the doctor immediately.

I said, "No way. I'm okay. I'll drive myself."

So I got in my car and drove to the doctor's office, where I was given various tests including an electrocardiogram and a blood test for heart enzymes. He said I seemed to be okay and told me to come back the next morning, after he had some time to examine previous electrocardiograms I had taken with a different doctor and get the blood test results.

The next day the doctor gave me another series of tests, including another EKG and a repeat of the blood work. I was still hooked up to the machine when he said, "You're having a heart attack."

I looked at him. I didn't believe him. I said, "You've got to be kidding."

He said no, he wasn't kidding, and he wanted me to go into a hospital right away.

I said, "I can't do that, I'm going to Los Angeles in two days to do the 'Mike Douglas Show.' Why don't you just give me a gross of nitroglycerine pills, and I'll go to LA, do the show, come back on a red-eye flight, and go into the hospital?"

The doctor frowned and said, "You can't do that. They don't let people who're having heart attacks get on planes."

I said, "You think I'm going to wear a sign that says, 'My name is Vinny Marino and I'm having a heart attack. Stay away, it's contagious'?"

He insisted. I went home. I phoned Vickie, and she rushed home. Then she phoned the doctor. I kept telling Vickie I was okay. I was in heavy denial: Who, me—a junkie? No way. Who, me—having a heart attack? Absolutely not.

Vickie was having none of it, and finally I agreed to go to the hospital but only after she cooked me some fried eggs and bacon. Looking back now, I can't believe I did that. I even put butter on the toast and salt on the eggs. I justified the meal by drinking a large glass of milk.

I was hospitalized for six weeks, during which time the doctor suggested that I might think about having surgery to remove a blockage in one artery. He said it wasn't absolutely necessary so I decided to postpone it. The truth is, I was scared, and I decided to go on a special diet instead. I found a doctor who said if I drank herb teas and ate properly, I could reverse the damage without surgery.

In time my fear went away, and I got on with life. A good thing, too, as there was so much to get back to.

While I was in the hospital, DSSH told us that we were losing one of our biggest money sources, Title XX funds. For several years, DSSH received $10 million in federal Title XX funds to purchase services the department was unable to provide from private agencies. Two-million dollars of this went to private treatment facilities such as Habilitat. We had been expecting $330,000 of this, based upon similar grants in recent years.

Then, in the fiscal year starting July 1, 1981, DSSH received only $510,000 for private treatment facilities. The other $1.5 million was being shifted to child abuse and elderly care services.

I had no argument with increasing these services, but approximately one-third of our total budget was comprised of Title XX money, money we used for half the yearly cost of the eighty residents who qualified and might otherwise be in prison or victimizing the community. And we weren't the only ones to suffer. The organization maintaining the state's federal methadone treatment program was also scheduled to lose funds. I still thought methadone was worse than heroin, and spoke out against it every chance I got. But I also knew the program had 110 addicts, and I didn't want to see them go "cold turkey" on the streets of Honolulu or return to heroin and, inevitably, the crime required to support the habit.

I wasn't entirely naive. I had known cutbacks like this were coming. The sixties were over, and dope fiends weren't in vogue any more. Even so, I thought a little more notice would have been nice so that Habilitat and the other local agencies could have prepared for the loss. I wrote letters to the papers expressing this point of view, and Dave George, my controller, went before the state legislature. Dave said our program would be seriously damaged unless the state made up the loss.

At first, the House of Representatives more or less went

along, approving $100,000—not enough to fill the gap, but more than I expected. When the subject went to the Senate for approval, our old friend Duke Kawasaki stood up. Oh-oh, I thought, here we go again.

He said Habilitat and its officers and staff (that's me) had a "profound contempt for the legislature." He said we had disregarded the audit entirely, and he said I was making $81,000 a year, counting fringe benefits, so Habilitat didn't deserve a penny.

On April 1 I sent a five-page letter to the Senate and House committees involved in our request. In the letter, I made it very clear that if we didn't get the money we needed, Habilitat was in deep, deep trouble. I also attached to the letter a long memo that I'd sent to DSSH the previous year, listing all the changes we'd made in direct response to the audit.

The changes were major, and Kawasaki should've known about them. As I said, I'd resigned voluntarily from the board, and several new members from outside Habilitat had been elected. My brother Frank was gone. New lines of communication were in place between Habilitat and government agencies, including DSSH and the Department of Health. The annual telethon had been dumped in favor of less costly fundraisers—another of their beefs. Plus I was paying a fair market rental on the house.

It didn't mean a thing. In recent months, Kawasaki had gotten a lot of unfortunate publicity regarding some big gambling debts he had in Las Vegas. I had nothing to do with it, but he thought I told the media to make him look bad. He continued his attack on us, and I went down to the state capitol with a bunch of my troops to stage a demonstration.

I said that if Habilitat and others had to turn their people out onto the streets, a lot of them would end up back in jail, which would cost the state more than giving us what we needed to remain open and fully functioning. As my troops marched up and down in front of the capitol building with signs that said "Habilitat, Cheaper Than Jail," I got ready for a press conference I had called. Representative Connie Chun came over to share a few choice words.

"We like Habilitat," she said, "we just don't like Vinny Marino. The best thing Habilitat can do is get him out of there."

Connie said one of the reasons she didn't like me was I failed to show up at a class at the University of Hawaii law school when she was a student there.

"Now the tables have turned," she said. "Six of the members of that class are upstairs in the legislature now."

I couldn't believe it. For *this* she was going to put dope fiends back on the streets?

I went ahead with my press conference and said it was a sad day when legislators admitted they were making such important decisions based on personality conflicts. I said, too, that I thought Habilitat would be around a hell of a lot longer than Duke Kawasaki and Connie Chun. I also mentioned that as far as I knew, Connie Chun's big claim to fame was that she was the proud owner of a 600-pound pig named Sooey, a pet she and her family insisted on keeping at home in their back yard. This went against all the zoning laws for her neighborhood, but when neighbors complained, the Chuns and the pig only got a lot of publicity, mainly here in Hawaii but also nationally.

I said, flippantly, "It seems to me that Connie has been riding her pig and has fallen off a few times and maybe landed on her head."

When the dust finally settled, the $100,000 we'd been promised by the House was whittled to $50,000. And by then it was late April. For nearly four months we'd been duking it out with Duke. I had better things to do.

One was handling the day-to-day business of getting people

to manage their lives and keeping the doors open so that would be possible. I felt it was time for a little lightheartedness so one of our new fund-raising ideas was a fashion show for dogs. The first week of June we had Habilitat's first, and last, annual "Canine Fashion Show" in a downtown Honolulu park. It didn't raise much money, but it did get us a lot of favorable publicity. And it helped raise the troops' spirits.

It was at this show we first sold homemade cookies. We used a recipe devised at Habilitat's kitchen when the cooks ran out of butter or margarine one day and substituted peanut butter. The name we gave them was awkward—"Hab-i-Cookie Champion Chips," but we sold every one we had and decided we were going to give Famous Amos some competition. So we turned the kitchen into a cookie factory between regular meals. By November, Habilitat was in the cookie business. Within a year we were producing and selling between forty and fifty thousand a month of what we renamed "24 KT Chip" cookies for a long list of vendors. And, by the way, Wally Amos became a good friend, helping us with our marketing. He even made his ovens available to us when we needed them.

Thanksgiving, Christmas, New Year's, and Habilitat's eleventh anniversary came and went quickly.

In 1982, we introduced another new event, taking over the Honolulu Club—a private social and athletic club downtown where Tom Selleck worked out regularly—for what we called a "Las Vegas Extravaganza." This was a black-tie benefit where people used "funny money" to play poker, blackjack, and craps while listening to free entertainment by Dick Jensen, Loyal Garner, Jan Brenner, Vic Leon, and others. Our total take at the end of the evening: $40,000; our net $25,000.

We also had our new institutional kitchen, dining room, and dorms to be thankful for, and we were planning a complete renovation of the other buildings ourselves. As a result, six of the most experienced reentry people and staff—headed by Frank Cockett with the help of a consultant named Herb Chock—started Habilitat Construction. This company later absorbed the landscaping and painting businesses and became known as Habilitat Services. Within four years it was grossing $1.5 million a year.

In 1982, though, that business was just getting started, and even if Christmas tree sales that summer were well ahead of the previous two years, we didn't have much reason to celebrate. We were still suffering from the loss of state and federal funds in 1981, and as each month passed, things got tighter and tighter.

In November, I found out that the state was late in making $150,000 in payments due for treating residents sent to us by the courts—all because we still refused to get out of Hab II. It looked like a bleak Christmas for Habilitat.

The next few days I spent in meetings with members of my key staff, trying to come up with ideas that would bail us out. We talked about giving workshops to people from other TC's, teaching them how to be less dependent on government funding. Even with all the handout money we had received— and suddenly weren't getting any more—we were still approaching the seventy percent mark in self-reliance. I thought if we shared our secrets, if we showed others how to raise money through telethons, services, Christmas trees, cookies, and other fund-raisers, we'd have another real money-maker on our hands. Send out brochures, sign up six hundred or so people at $1,000 apiece, and after expenses we'd clear an easy half million.

I also sent letters to the commissioners of the National Football League, the National Basketball Association, and the National Baseball League. I offered to lead seminars on drug abuse for any team of the commissioner's choice, without cost.

I said, "I will explain why people use drugs and tell what drugs can really do to athletes. I will dismiss the myth of recreational drug use and lay out in a clear and concise manner how anyone can avoid getting involved with drugs no matter how socially acceptable drugs seem to be in any peer group.

"All of this will be done in a way that will not demean the players or give them the impression that they are being 'lectured.' They will enjoy the workshop, and they will thank you for introducing them to it. If you like what I do, then we will sit down and negotiate, at a nominal fee, my doing the same workshop with all the other teams. If you don't like what I do, of course, we shake hands and say aloha."

Letters were sent to Mike Wallace at "Sixty Minutes" and to several other TV shows, suggesting me as a guest and Habilitat as the subject for a feature story. Other letters were sent to national lecture bureaus.

Whatever value these and many other ideas had, none produced any immediate cash. (Too bad about the sports; later events showed they needed help. They should've listened.)

I looked at Habilitat's latest financial report. Hab Services were operating at a small profit, but the cookie business was barely breaking even and unable to grow because we'd reached capacity with Habilitat's kitchen. (Another of our pressing needs: money to build a professional bakery in our warehouse.) The only real moneymaker was the Christmas tree operation, which we expected to net $100,000. The only trouble was that most of the trees were prepaid at the time of the order, and the money had been spent long ago.

I sat and reviewed the past two years, thinking about Kawasaki's audit and the telethon money we lost because of it and the end of the telethon as a reliable, annual fund-raiser because it had run out of steam plus the audit influenced us to drop it. Then came the loss of Title XX funds, another heavy-duty blow. After that, Kawasaki slapped us around again and made sure that our funding request was cut from $330,000 to $50,000. On top of this, the National Institute on Drug Abuse (NIDA), one of the leading federal agencies funding educational and treatment programs, announced that it was cutting all its funding to Habilitat as well as to all other centers locally and nationally. At the time, NIDA had been giving us nearly $300,000 annually.

That did it. In a year's time, we had lost more than $600,000. After many front-line meetings with my key staff— and I mean *many* meetings—and after spending hours in my office studying Habilitat's table of organization to pinpoint positions we could live without if we had to, I carefully made a list of thirty-one people, nearly fifty percent of my staff.

I knew it would be easier to function *with* these people, but I also knew that if me and my other staff picked up the slack, we could survive. And if we didn't let that many go, no way could we survive at all. This was extremely painful for me, and I called in each person and explained to him or her personally that it had nothing to do with performance; it was simply a matter of keeping the doors open. I said if the situation changed, I would rehire as many as I possibly could. It wasn't easy, but everyone understood.

The hell of it was, this didn't seem to change anything. We had done well with new fund-raisers, the businesses were picking up, and the drastic staff cutbacks helped, of course, but we still didn't regain the momentum we lost or manage to climb out of the red.

After meeting with Dave George again, I called another staff meeting.

I said, "I don't have very good news. I'll be honest with you. If something miraculous doesn't happen fast, we won't be able to make the January bills. According to what Dave just told me, if we don't come up with $268,000 by January 15 . . ."

I didn't finish the sentence. I didn't have to.

I don't think I ever sounded so negative. Vickie reminded me that she had been talking with a guy on the East Coast whose best friend's son had just entered the program. He'd said that if we got the kid off drugs, he'd give us $100,000.

Vickie said, "Why not ask him for the money now? Except, don't ask him for a hundred, ask for $268,000."

I said I didn't know if he'd go for it because he had said he wanted results first. Later I met with Vickie and Frank Cockett and said, "How am I gong to close on him? I never met him. His friend's son hasn't been here very long, only a few weeks. How . . ."

Vickie politely interrupted me and said she'd be right back. She came back a few minutes later with another proposal. In this one, Habilitat was asking for another $200,000.

I said, "Hey, wait a minute. I just asked you how I was going to close for $268,000 and you give me a proposal for $200,000 more? You want me to ask for $468,000? What are you—a comedian?"

She said, "Why not go for the whole enchilada?"

I looked at Vickie as if she'd lost her mind. She was grinning. Frank started to smile. Finally, I started to smile, too. In a couple of minutes, we were all laughing.

"What the fuck," I said, "let's go for it!"

I called my secretary in and asked her to place a long distance call to the East Coast.

"This is Vinnie Marino at Habilitat," I said, when I got the gentleman on the line. (He and his foundation asked to remain anonymous.) "I'm going to be in your neighborhood in a couple of weeks, the end of November, and I wondered if we might get together."

He said his schedule was full, but he was available December 5, 1982. I said I could juggle my calendar, and after hanging up, I told my secretary to book me a flight.

I turned back to Vickie and Frank.

"What the fuck!" I said. And we all started laughing again.

≥●

Chapter Eighteen

SELF-SUFFICIENCY, AT LAST!

Before leaving Hawaii, I spent a lot of energy trying to figure out how I was going to close on a guy I had never met. The easiest part of any sale is always the actual sale itself. It's the getting ready, the psyching up that's hard. I knew that what the mind of man can conceive, he can do. I also knew that once you believe you can do something, the rest is history.

But I was still nervous. After all, $468,000 is not chump change. To go up to someone you've never met and ask him for almost half a million dollars when he doesn't even know why you've requested the meeting—well, to be honest, I was worried. An awful lot was riding on this, and I didn't want to blow it.

In November, there's a five-hour time difference between Hawaii and Washington. I wanted to be clear eyed and as sharp as possible so I left two days ahead of the meeting. I figured that would also give me time to prepare my pitch and I'd be able to rest. But I was wrong about that. With the time change and the cold, wet December weather, plus my anxiety, I couldn't sleep. I couldn't stop my mind from racing.

We had plans to meet for dinner in a restaurant not far from my hotel. About an hour and a half beforehand, one of his associates called to say he was in the lobby. He suggested we have a cup of coffee in the hotel and then drive to the restaurant. I put on my jacket and went downstairs.

We liked each other right away. He made me feel at ease. When he asked me what it was I wanted, I told him. I gave him a short version of what I had expected to give later over dinner. I told him that two hundred people were depending on me and if I was successful, it'd be a happy Christmas and new year. If not, we were in very, very deep trouble — we'd have to close up shop.

He seemed sympathetic so I asked him if he thought there was any area I should stay away from.

He said, "Just be honest, Vinny, that's all."

He paused a minute, then said, "By the way, how much are you going to ask him for?"

I told him the amount, $468,000.

He didn't even blink an eye. "No big thing," he said. "You have to understand, my friend's son is very important to him."

He was paged to go to the phone and soon we were on our way to the restaurant. We got there and were taken to our table.

He said, "Relax, Vinny. I'll help you."

A few minutes later, when his boss entered the restaurant, it was obvious that everyone knew him. We shook hands and after some small talk, he said he wanted to order. I was thinking,

"How can you think of food at a time like this?" But of course I didn't say anything.

Over espresso, we got down to business. I made my pitch. I went over the whole thing from soup to nuts. This was the greatest role of my career, and I got very emotional to the point where I cried. I told him about the political skullduggery. I told him about all the bullshit and how much of my life was Habilitat. I told him about the troops and how much we wanted, needed, to be independent so we could kick the establishment in the ass and get on with what we knew best, helping people.

He looked at me and said, "Okay, how much do you need?"

I felt as if I had half of the sand in Hawaii in my mouth. I could hear machine guns and bombs going off.

I cleared my throat and said, "$468,000."

I actually saw the numbers move in front of my eyes as I said them, like $468,000 floating across the room in neon lights.

He didn't blink an eye.

I had brought the two proposals that Vickie wrote, and he asked for them. I told him one was for $268,000, and the other for $200,000. He nodded and ordered another cup of coffee.

He would've made a great poker player. I couldn't read him at all. We talked small talk, and then he said he had to go meet his business partners. He said he would drop me at my hotel on the way.

It was only five minutes away. I wanted another hour to go over my pitch again, but I didn't have the time so I said what was on my mind.

"What do you think, how does it look? I'm a big boy, it's hard to hurt my feelings. On a scale of ten, what shot do we have? What are the odds?"

He matter-of-factly said, "Seventy percent."

I knew that didn't mean we were home free yet. I knew that didn't happen until the check—if he gave us one—cleared the bank, but I thanked him like I've never thanked anyone in my life. I thanked him for the youngest to the oldest resident at Habilitat. I thanked him for the newest to the oldest staff member. I thanked him for the board of directors. I thanked him for the state of Hawaii and parts of Guam and was about to thank him for Tahiti and Bora Bora when he interrupted me.

He said, "I'll give you an answer at noon tomorrow."

The next morning I must've worn half the carpet's life away, walking up and down, waiting for the phone to ring. Noon, twelve-thirty, one o'clock, and no phone call.

Back in Hawaii people were waiting for me to call. I looked at my watch and figured out the time difference and saw my troops finishing breakfast and starting the morning meeting. I could hear them singing songs and laughing.

Finally at quarter to two I said the hell with this, and phoned *him*.

I said, "Hi. I was out of the room. Did you call? I may not have gotten the message."

He said, "Look, Vinny, I've been involved in meetings about this and that. I'll get back to you by four o'clock."

Four o'clock comes and no phone call. Finally at four-thirty he calls me up and says, "How you doing?"

I laugh and answer, "Hey, let's not get into that. I'm a little tired from a lot of exercise pacing back and forth, which is probably good for my heart. But what's the bottom line? Can you help us?"

He said, "I can give you $400,000."

I had to sit down on the bed. I said, "I don't know if you realize but this really bails us out."

We talked for a few more minutes, and after I hung up, I

called Hawaii. Vickie was running the meeting. I told her the news, and she told everybody in the room. I could hear them all scream.

To this day, I will never be able to repay this guy. If not for him, Habilitat could in no way, shape, or form be in the kind of position we're in now. What we did was capitalize on something negative, the audit, and turn it into something extremely positive. In the end, the audit worked for us.

When I got back to Hawaii, a reporter for the *Sun Press* interviewed me. One of the questions he asked was how I felt about the city vetoing our application for $160,000 in federal Community Development Block Grant funds. With the check for $400,000 arriving any day from Washington, I really didn't give a shit so I told the reporter that I was, as of now, giving up asking the government for anything.

I said, "It's like dealing with idiots. I try to conduct my business honorably and amicably, but when you deal with idiots you have to resort to acting like an idiot."

I didn't tell the media anything about the big check. Why should I? The press hardly ever gave me a break during the audit. Why should I give them one now? Certainly I wouldn't give them one they could turn around and distort. Because that's exactly what they would've done. If I'd have said we got a private donation that big, the media would've written us off. They would've said we obviously didn't need any public support now that we had a millionaire angel paying the bills. They wouldn't print it when the Red Cross or the Boy Scouts or any other organization got a big check. With us, we would have come out the heavies. And the legislature probably would've called for another audit—this time to see if we were a cult blackmailing parent and friends of our residents into emptying their bank accounts.

The money from Washington arrived in three installments.

The first was a personal check for $188,000, and it arrived by Federal Express on December 31, New Year's eve. I remember sending one of my troops to the airport to get the envelope. I also tried to get my bank to open the next day to accept the deposit, to no avail. The second installment, a personal check for $12,000 and a check for $100,000 from his foundation, arrived January 10. The final $100,000 arrived in early April.

I got into my last pissing contest with the legislature a month after. It started February 16 when Ken Kiyabu, the chairman of the House finance committee, and six other members of his committee were on a fact-finding tour of the state hospital, otherwise known as the den of iniquity. They also paid a surprise visit to Hab II, which we had still refused to vacate. One of my assistant directors told them that the visit was not cleared by me so they would have to leave.

Kiyabu asked, "Are you saying that state legislators can't come on state property to look at a state facility?"

My assistant director said, "Yes, that's right."

Kiyabu looked at his pals and said, "Well, we'll see you down the road when the session starts, and you guys come and ask for money."

I thought it ironic that on the same property was Windward University and a private alcoholic treatment program called Hina Mauka, which they did *not* visit. I guess it was just another case where they wanted to break our balls so they singled us out.

The next day I told the media that the legislators were, in fact, trespassing. They weren't visiting a state facility; they were making a surprise visit on a private, nonprofit institution that happened to be occupying a building owned by the state. There's a big difference, and tenants have a right to be told in advance when the "landlord" is coming to look around. I told the press that legislators were welcome at Habilitat any time.

They just had to call first. I also told them that if Ken Kiyabu ever offered me any money, he could stick it up his nose.

Now, a legislative hearing was scheduled for two days later, on the nineteenth. I said I was going to be there. I wouldn't tell them what I was going to say, but I did warn them: "I'm coming out of a tree, and you should be there to catch my act!"

The nineteenth was a Saturday, which is generally a slow news day, and the papers and TV knew that good old Vinny was always ripe for a headline so they all showed up. I went down there all dressed up, and there the legislators were, sitting back and relaxed, with all the TV lights off. As soon as I entered, technicians from Channels 2, 4, and 9 got up and got ready to put the lights on.

I had two other staff with me, and when we sat down in the rear, the cameramen sat down too. The chairman of the committee called the meeting to order, and except for us, everybody stood up and moved to the big table in the front of the room. The chairman asked everyone to give their names, their positions, and the organizations they represented.

As I sat there, listening, I thought, there are enough titles around here to rule the goddamned world.

Finally I stood up and said, "If it pleases the chairman, I'd like to have the floor."

When I said that, the TV cameramen jumped to their feet, and the lights came on.

I said, "I'm looking around this room at all these programs and titles, and I really wonder what they do. I think that's funny because I've been here in Hawaii twelve years, and this is a small state, and I'm an expert in my field. And I *still* have no idea what these programs are doing, nor why they charge as much as they charge, nor why they should be funded. Does anybody here know what they do?

"These people should go out and earn their own money or at least match government money dollar-for-dollar. The legislature should audit them, the same as you did us. I find it strange that Habilitat was the only program in the history of Hawaii to be audited. Don't you care where the money is going?

"How much is going for salaries? How much for food? How much for utilities? How much for vehicles? This is the taxpayer's money. If it was coming out of your pocket, you'd want to know."

I paused and Senator Ben Cayetano said, "Vinny, is it true that you told Ken Kiyabu to shove his money up his ass?"

That got a very big laugh, and I tried not to smile as I said, "No, sir, I told him his nose. You know me, Ben. I would never talk like that."

That got another big laugh, and then he said, "Vinny, over the years, we've been good to you."

I said, "There are some legislators—Ben, you're one of them—that have been very good to us, who understand what Habilitat is all about. I'm not so sure about some of the others."

With that, I left the hearing room. The television cameras followed me outside, and I continued to let the other programs have it. That night, I was all over the evening TV news and the next day in the Sunday paper.

Then, later, the legislature offered us $67,000, and I turned it down. I told them to give it to senior citizens; they needed it more than Habilitat.

A week after the hearing and our declaration of independence, we introduced a new fund-raising idea. This was our Family Exposition, a two-day event held in the Neal Blaisdell Center Exhibition Hall, formerly the HIC. We'd been planning it for three months—as always doing something first and then learning how to do it as we went along. Our acquisitions

department had been on the phones every day, hustling products we could give away for door prizes. Eventually, we got
enough free musical instruments, jewelry, clothing, and
household goods to give away $50 in prizes every ten minutes,
plus free trips to Disneyland and a 1983 Nissan Sentra.

Sheldon Klotzman, a cocaine addict from Baltimore, was
instrumental in selling two hundred booths to local businesses. We also booked twenty hours of free entertainment by
dozens of top local performers. We had videogames, more than
fifteen different food locations, martial arts demonstrations,
aerobic dancing, wandering magicians, and clowns. It was
good, wholesome family entertainment—with the emphasis
on the word *family*.

At two o'clock in the morning on the day we were to open
the doors, something happened that made us all want to can-
cel it. One of our most popular residents, Richard Medeiros,
who was nineteen, was unloading food cases from a truck at
our warehouse when he collapsed.

He and some of the other guys had just made the last
delivery of supplies to the exhibition hall. Two of my guys
trained in CPR tried to bring him around while taking him to
Castle Hospital about four miles away.

Richard was from the Big Island. He never had a serious
problem—he just needed some direction. He was a confused
kid, and he came to Habilitat through the courts. He fit right
in, and pretty soon he had one of the best attitudes. He'd been
in the program for about two-and-a-half years and was very
close to graduating.

A little after three o'clock in the morning, I received a
phone call. I was told that Richard was in the hospital and that
he had died. I dressed quickly and rushed to the hospital.
There was Richard—pale and lifeless. I hugged and kissed him
and then phoned the facility.

Habilitat's Family Expo always offer hundreds of things to see and do.

"Call a general meeting, immediately," I said. "Wake everybody up. I'm on my way over."

That was one of the hardest GMs I ever held. It was a major shock. Everybody loved Richard. I told them there was no lease: You take every day as it comes, make the best of it, because that's all you're going to get—one day at a time. I talked about death, and I talked about Richard. I said that man's potential to do was limitless, and Richard believed that. He came to Habilitat an introvert, and in time he balanced that out. He became an extrovert, the middle man wherever he could help. I said we had a lot to learn from Richard.

I acknowledged that we were sad. And I said that as much as I, personally, wanted in one way to say the hell with it, the Family Exposition was going ahead as planned. Not only that, it was going to be a success. I said that if anybody wanted to get some sleep, now was the time. If not, it was okay to stay up and talk. Maybe we'd even get an early start and make sure that everything was ready at the hall.

Two days later, preliminary figures showed we'd made a profit of about $20,000, which is considered a big success for that sort of thing in the first year.

Three days later we held services for Richard. All of us wore Habilitat tee-shirts, and I gave the eulogy. I made it very clear that we were there to celebrate Richard's life. We all expressed our condolences to his family. Then, sadly, we returned to Habilitat.

Several months passed before we finally got the cause of Richard's death. When the story first appeared in the papers, there were many rumors that it could've been an overdose. That's bullshit. I'm afraid any program will never completely overcome this kind of idiotic thinking. And this fact wasn't helped any when the papers failed to print anything about the medical examiner's report: Richard had died of an aneurism in the brain.

Five thousand copies of my autobiography, *Vinny,* arrived in March. Some color proofs of the cover had come in before Christmas, and it was rare when I didn't have one with me to show all my friends. On the front was a picture of me, looking serious and a little angelic, almost as if I were praying with my eyes open. You bet I was praying, praying people would like the book and get its message that if I could survive, anyone can.

On the back of the cover were quotes praising the book from James Wechsler, the *New York Post* columnist who wrote about me over the years; Bob Newhart, who remained a friend and supporter; and Senator Dan Inouye.

Inside the book I ran my last mug shots, taken by the New York police department at my last arrest, my "rap sheet" (list of my criminal arrests), and my undesirable discharge from the U.S. Army. I always figured they were credentials to run Habilitat. Just like lawyers, doctors, and other professionals frame their diplomas and certificates and put them on their office wall, I had these three items on display in my office.

The book was eight years in the making. To tell the truth, it was an albatross around my neck. Writing is not my field, and it was difficult.

First I worked on it alone, but at the same time I had to run the program, raise money to keep the doors open, and everything else so I could never work on it for long. Then because it was so hard, reliving my life, I sometimes got so mad I would throw the damned thing against the wall. Then it would go back into a drawer for six months.

I don't even remember the names of all the writers I tried to work with. Finally, in frustration, I decided to finish the book alone, changing and adding things until I almost drove myself nuts.

The worst time was between getting the first dust jackets, in December 1982, and when the finished books finally arrived

Vinny's autobiography up to the birth of Habilitat.

three months later. I was a nervous wreck. One of my consultants, who had published close to a dozen books himself, told me putting out a book was like having a baby. He was right. I hadn't been that anxious since little Vickie was born.

It's funny because at first I hadn't wanted to write that book at all. I wanted to write *this* book, a history of Habilitat. But several of my "rabbis" thought it would be better if I wrote the story of my life as a junkie first. They said it would give the background to Habilitat, tell the story that led up to it, and so make more sense. In other words, before I could write the story of Habilitat, I had to tell the story of Vinny Marino.

It was painful, but at last the finished book was in my hands. Now it was time to sell it. I figured this book could be the hook that would get Habilitat the attention it needed and deserved, but we'd have to sell the hell out of it, the same way we sold cookies and Christmas trees. And this time, we'd sell from coast to coast.

We got national distribution in the Waldenbooks and B. Dalton chains, which is unheard of for a book not published by one of the major New York companies. I hired Rogers and Cowan, a big publicity firm headquartered in Beverly Hills, to book me on a national publicity tour. This company was known as "the General Motors of publicity." The year before they'd taken a Spanish singer named Julio Iglesias, who was then unknown in this country, and turned him into an American household word (sort of the answer to Mick Jagger for Middle America). I was hoping the company could work a little of the same magic for me. They also had offices in New York and London and had been in business for more than thirty years, with many corporate accounts besides all the biggest stars. All I knew was I was in the hands of pros.

Maybe because I didn't sing, I don't know, but at the end of the tour I was still a little less well-known than Julio. Truthfully,

Rogers and Cowan did a great job. I started out in May and did twenty-seven cities in eight weeks, giving more than a hundred interviews from sea to shining sea—an experience I don't recommend to anyone.

It was also on this tour that something happened to affect Habilitat as much as our generous donor from Washington, D.C. had. I was in a hotel room somewhere, watching television, when I saw a commercial for the *National Enquirer*. The cover of the *Enquirer* that week showed a picture of Griffin O'Neal, and the headline asked "Why isn't Ryan O'Neal's son smiling?" At the time, I'm not even sure I knew the actor had a son, and I didn't much care either.

The next day after I called my office in Hawaii, I changed my mind when I was told that Griffin was a resident.

Less than a month later, after my return to Hawaii, I got a phone call from Dave Donnelly, the gossip columnist for the evening paper in Honolulu. He said he had been called by a Los Angeles stringer for *People* magazine about Ryan O'Neal's son being in a drug rehab center in Hawaii. Dave told the guy from *People*, "Well, if it's true, he must be in my friend Vinny's place, Habilitat."

People asked Dave, "You know this Vinny?"

Dave said he did, and the stringer asked him to call me to confirm the rumor that he had picked up in Hollywood from one of Griffin's friends.

Dave was a longtime friend, and I didn't want to lie to him. I said, "Can you take off your business hat?"

He said he could, and I said, "Yes, Griffin O'Neal is a resident. He's been here a little more than a month. But I need some time before anything is done so I can inform Ryan."

Dave went along, and I told Dave I'd call him in no more than two days—then I started calling Ryan's home in California. I hadn't reached him when, the next day, Dave phoned me again. He said he had heard from *People* magazine again, and they were sending one of their top writers out from New York because the story was too big for the LA stringer.

Dave said, "My advice to you is they're going to run the story anyway so you better be ready."

I still couldn't find Ryan so I spoke to Griffin and asked him what he wanted to do. He felt bad about the whole situation, especially how he made his father look. He was worried that they'd probably rehash the same garbage that was in the *Enquirer.*

Griffin said, "Let the reporter come out. I'll speak to him. Maybe I can clean this thing up and put it in proper perspective."

I figured Griffin was old enough to make a decision, and I told him I'd make sure that I was with him, along with some of my key staff.

Griffin was anxious to get his version across, that it really wasn't his father's fault when Ryan punched him and knocked out two front teeth. He was just doing what any father would've done. It was as if Ryan was saying, "I'll see my son in a body cast from beating him up before I see him at a funeral because of an overdose of drugs."

The story appeared in *People* in August 1983. On the cover was a picture of Ryan O'Neal with his fiance Farrah Fawcett, plus a picture of Griffin, with the headline, "Life with Father: A volatile upbringing leads to violence and drugs for Ryan O'Neal's son." The story went on for six pages but revealed little about Griffin's days at Habilitat. It was about growing up in Hollywood.

People told Griffin's whole story in great detail. As teenagers, he and his sister, Tatum, had been left alone a lot of the time. He dropped out of school, and when he wasn't acting in a movie, he partied, getting wasted on Quaaludes and alcohol. Eventually he got in trouble with the police.

When Griffin was given his induction interview at Habilitat, he was asked what he wanted.

Griffin said, "I want your help."

The guys doing the interview said, "Good, you're going to get it. Now what can you give us?"

Griffin told them about his piano playing talents, his two movies, and named a few of his famous Malibu friends.

One of the residents looked at him straight in the eye and said, "If you're so fucking terrific, why don't you whistle through those beautiful front teeth of yours?"

Then they started shouting at him, telling him he was a piece of shit, and Griffin started crying.

Griffin hated Habilitat at first. He didn't like having his head shaved. He didn't like being told what to do. He didn't like being watched all the time, and he didn't like being called a punk by people he thought were inferior.

The turning point came a month after his first visit from Ryan and Farrah. He walked off the premises and tried to call a girlfriend in LA and his father. Neither was home. One of my staff, looking out of a window at Hab II, saw Griffin in a phone booth nearby. He went after Griffin and brought him in a car to Hab I.

Griffin was told to sit on a tall stool reserved for people on their way into or out of the program. Coming back into the program, we called these people "splitees." He was still resisting the program and hating it. One of his friends came strolling by, a guy he knew from Malibu.

This guy was on a "talking ban" with Griffin, meaning they were not allowed to communicate. The kid stopped dead in his tracks and opened his mouth to talk to Griffin.

Several others nearby told him, "No! Don't break the ban. Let the asshole go. Let him split."

Griffin's friend said, "Whoa! That's my friend."

He walked up to Griffin and said, "You going some-where?" He kept talking. After a few minutes, Griffin was cry-ing. He decided to stay in the program.

The following June, on the anniversary of his entering Habilitat, *People* ran a follow-up story. Again it was a cover story, and this time the title read, "Fighting Back: For the first time, Griffin O'Neal tells the wrenching story of his struggle to win dad Ryan's love—and to beat drugs." Inside, next to the story, was a full-page picture of Griffin standing on the beach near the facility, wearing a Habilitat tee-shirt.

That's when the phones at Habilitat started ringing off the hook.

Chapter Nineteen

FORECASTING THE FUTURE

It took Griffin nine months to give up his resistance to our program and do it Habilitat's way. After that, it was a piece of cake. He soon went into reentry and joined Hab Services where he installed porous rock-and-epoxy driveways and patio decks. Finally, after two years, he graduated, in the summer of 1985.

When I was out promoting my book, I had to hire a publicity firm to get bookings on national TV shows, and at that time I didn't get on several of the top shows. Now after the follow-up article on Griffin in *People*, those shows were calling *me*. The difference was when I was promoting my autobiography, I did the shows alone. Now everybody wanted me and Griffin together.

"Today," "CBS Morning News," (where one of the reporters,

Maria Shriver, was a personal friend of Tatum O'Neal's and did a very sympathetic interview), "Good Morning America," "Larry King," "Michael Jackson"—you name the show, they called. I knew if I said yes, we'd be criticized. Some people would say I was exploiting Griffin and his family. We also knew Griffin would catch some heavy flak. After all, his family had suffered enough living through the experience. Why should they now have to watch all the dirty laundry hung out to dry on coast to coast TV?

We did the shows anyway. Griffin checked it out with his dad, and Ryan gave his okay, although naturally he did not want to take part in any of the interviews. In the end, I figured it was good for Griffin and for Habilitat.

I wanted Griffin to remain in Hawaii after his graduation because I didn't think he was ready to return to Hollywood's fast lane. At first he agreed, but soon he returned and started making movies again.

Even so, he stayed in touch and continued to give interviews about his experience at Habilitat and what it did for him. Through the rest of 1985 and into 1986, many national magazines and TV shows ran features about drugs and celebrities and their kids. And every time, Griffin and Habilitat were part of the story. I continued to do interviews, too, and made more than fifteen national appearances that year.

All this made the Habilitat phones even more popular, especially with our new toll-free number (1-800-USA-2525). We had this number put in as a crisis intervention, prevention, and referral hotline so troubled kids and parents could call Habilitat for help.

By the end of 1985, our population was soaring. Some new residents were the children of famous Hollywood stars or producers, and we even had some stars themselves. (Somehow the media never learned of this.) At the same time, we were still getting residents from the court system not only in Hawaii, but also from throughout the United States so the background mix was much the same.

The troops were getting younger though. From the time we started the house in Kailua, we always had a lot of teenagers, but the average age was about twenty-two or twenty-three. Now it was dropping as more and more younger kids came in.

As a result, I reduced the length of the program for the younger ones. Older people, with ten or fifteen years of steady drug abuse, you're not going to turn them around in a year or eighteen months—it takes longer. With the young ones, it's different. I also worry about these young kids getting institutionalized. That can happen even in a year. When they experience the first real structured environment with conditional love, they grab it the way they would've grabbed a family life at home, if it had been that way.

Another thing, the drugs today are different. When I was using, it was heroin, and the only way that I deviated was to mix it with cocaine (speedballs). We used barbiturates when the quality of heroin dropped. In essence, a drug addict had some scruples. He definitely knew what he was using.

I just interviewed a kid the other day; he had three earrings and a punk hairdo. A real wisenheimer know-it-all kid. I asked him what he used. He said, "Pot, acid, coke, and Kiwi shoe polish." I'm not kidding. These kids will do anything to get high. They sniff aerosol cans, typewriter white-out, and oil-based felt-tip marker pens.

They also mix drugs. You don't get just one drug dependency anymore. Now it's two or three—pot and beer, or pot and wine and crack. By comparison, heroin habits are easy. Give me a regular dope fiend—heroin and maybe a little coke—I can deal with that. Kids with their brains fried by

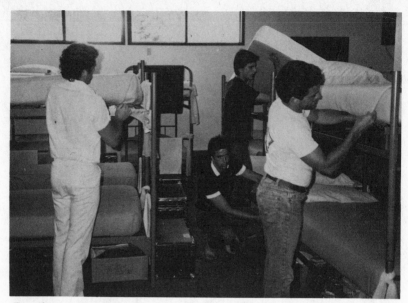

Residents straightening up the dorm. Responsbility and accountability are very important.

Morning meeting.

hallucinogenics—that makes it difficult. Those are the ones you find in the back wards of state mental institutions.

Habilitat now does some heavy medical screening. In fact I sometimes feel like Marcus Welby. We will not take anyone with AIDS antibodies. There are programs on the mainland that will, and they farm the residents out to a hospital when they develop full-blown AIDS. I refuse to jeopardize the other residents.

I think a big difference in why Habilitat is successful is that I'm still very much involved with the troops. With mainland programs, the directors have only a casual relationship with the troops. Instead, they're into the three-piece suits, the attaché case, the administration. Most can't even identify their residents by name. I can put a name with every face and tell you that person's story. I like to be in the front lines. I still conduct the dissipations (long encounter groups), the marathons, and the staff games. Also I run my own tutorials, which I conduct with post reentry and staff trainees. Whatever I teach that group is carried right down the line to the rest of the troops by my staff. I also conduct most of the general meetings.

Some people say I've mellowed with the years. Some say the heart attack did it. Others say it's because Habilitat is successful, and we don't need the publicity now that we have people like Burt Reynolds, Dick Clark, Dom DeLuise, and others endorsing us on national TV spots.

Nothing could be further from the truth. I'm only keeping my mouth shut because I don't have the time to do otherwise. I was spending too much energy fighting the department of health and the prison system, Koolau, some of the psychiatrists here, when I could've been doing something else. In a way it was fun because it was something different, and it gave me a chance to vent my frustration and make some changes. I also *had* to fight in those days—to survive.

But now I don't have to spend a lot of energy worrying about being evicted or being able to live in a particular neighborhood. Now I can spend whatever energies I have with my troops. It's more productive, and it's less of a hassle for me.

I don't think anything's changed, by the way. Here we are, going into our sixteenth year, and not only are the things I'm against still with us, they're worse. Let me tell you a story that unless you live in Hawaii, you won't believe. And you'll only believe it in Hawaii because it happened, it was in the newspapers and on TV.

Early this year, they discovered a man in the women's prison. So what's news about that? This man was an *inmate*, and he'd been living in the women's prison undetected for several weeks. None of the guards or prison administrators even noticed! I think that's hilarious. I also think it shows how good a job the people in the prison are doing.

The truth is, the prison system and the mental health system have been set up to fail because if they succeeded—if people actually got well or were rehabilitated—the system would self-destruct. That means one hell of a lot of people would be out of work.

Ossining, New York, was probably a nice little town until they brought Sing Sing Prison in. When they built that prison, they had to find people to staff it. Then they had to build houses for the staff people and schools for their kids—plus banks, stores, gas stations, theaters, bowling alleys, everything a town needs. Finally you've got a booming little city. If Sing Sing did what it was supposed to do, they'd have to close it down because eventually there wouldn't be any more prisoners to rehabilitate. Then what happens to the town and all the people who work there?

It's the same way here in Hawaii. Right now, they're building two more prisons because the ones we have are overcrowded. By the time the new ones are ready, of course, they'll be overcrowded, too. And then they'll build some more. More prisons means more jobs. As long as the prisons fail, there will be more and more of them instead of less.

Sometimes I don't think *anything* works in the prison system today. If you were a tavern owner who had a fraction of the fights and knifings that go on in a prison in a year, they'd close you down forever. Meanwhile the prisons go sailing along.

For years there's been talk about the death penalty and the reason for having it is to serve as a deterrent. For me, the only one it deters is the person they put away. If they televised the executions on every channel and showed the agony of killing someone, and everybody had to watch, *then* it might be a deterrent.

Mental hospitals are no better. They keep their people deeply tranquilized to make the staff jobs easy. This way, they're too fucked up to do any damage. Of course, they're also too fucked up for anyone to learn why they were crazy— or even *if* they were crazy—in the first place.

For years now, the Hawaii state hospital hasn't even been accredited. They get around it by giving the hospital "temporary" accreditation so they'll be eligible for funding.

And the doctors in prisons are the worst you'll find anywhere. Every doctor I met in prison, I think he came directly from Auschwitz. I don't think any of them in the prison system or the mental health system could create a private practice. Nobody'd go to them.

The way I see it, 15 to 20 percent of the people in prison are totally insane. They belong in a maximum security mental institution of some kind. Another 15 to 20 percent are incorrigible. They've seen too many James Cagney movies. We don't have a war going on now, and I think this group could be put in empty military brigs.

The other 60 or 70 percent can be helped, and they should be farmed out to programs like Habilitat. In this state alone, we need fifteen to twenty more Habilitats.

Over the years, people have asked me if I'd like to have more facilities, maybe on some of the other islands. My answer is, "Absolutely not." There'd be too much wear and tear on my brain. People from outside the system, like me, are not welcome. How do you think I got my heart attack, playing with a yo-yo? It was from trying to keep the morons off Habilitat's back.

I've always wondered if the state had been more cooperative and less threatened by us, how many more people we could've helped. I've also always wondered why the state didn't take advantage of Habilitat. The federal government says we're the most successful and creative rehabilitation program in the entire country. We have a recovery rate three times the national average! You'd think a state would be proud of that. But, no, Hawaii went the other way and tried to put us out of business. They hit me with everything they could.

I think that if they had taken care of their own problems in the prisons and the state hospital, they wouldn't have had so much time to come after us. I also think that if they hadn't been such a bunch of idiots, they might have been tougher to handle. If I'd come up against anyone intelligent, I would have had a harder time. After all, Habilitat occupied the state hospital building—Hab II—for thirteen years when all we had was a one-year lease. What kind of landlord would put up with that?

By the way, the reason the state expressed for trying to evict us for so long was that they needed the space. As I write this, it's over two years since we left, and the building is still empty.

If all this sounds a bit downbeat, that's because it is—not for us but for the rest of the state, as well as the rest of the

United States. Habilitat will continue to do what it does long after I'm gone. And the country will continue to do what it does. The people running Habilitat have been trained at Habilitat; the penologists and mental health people are trained within the system. Habilitat will continue to succeed; the system will continue to fail.

We've had a lot of support from the people of Hawaii, and we're grateful. Without the people here, we wouldn't have made it. But while they have helped us, they have also turned their backs on the prison and hospital system. It's almost as if they didn't care about how their tax money was being spent. If you bought a new TV set, and it didn't work, would you say, "Oh, well!" and put it in the corner and forget about it? Hell, no, you'd take it back and get a set that worked or get your money back.

When it comes to your tax dollars, though, it's different. The money goes out and nothing comes back that works. And you shake your head and say, "Oh, well!"

People used to get upset about such things. They rallied, like they did in the sixties about Vietnam, and there was change. Today it's harder to organize, I guess. People are more apathetic. Today it's, "I got mine, you get yours."

Habilitat stands for the way America *used* to be when the settlers came here and shared all they had. Nobody went hungry. No one got fat, either. Today it looks like everybody wants to get fat.

I know that Habilitat doesn't work for everybody, but I know that it *can* work for anybody. I also know that as the great Yogi Berra once said, "It ain't over until it's over."

Chapter Twenty

OLD FRIENDS TODAY

In my first book, in which I told how I managed to survive a life of crime and drugs, I talked about many escapades I had with a guy named Hooks. In that book, I told how it turned out for me — clean and starting a rehabilitation survival school of my own — but I forgot to tell about Hooks.

Since reading it, thousands of people have asked me, "Whatever happened to Hooks?"

Well, I'm happy to report that Hooks came to Hawaii. Following a painful detox from methadone, he entered Habilitat and graduated. Then he joined our staff. When I closed advertising specialties, though, I had to let him go. He is still married, to someone on Habilitat's staff, and works in Honolulu.

There are a lot of characters in Habilitat's story you may
be wondering about, and I promised myself I wasn't going to
leave their stories unfinished this time. I don't want to spend
the next decade with people coming up to me saying, "Whatever happened to the guy who thought he was a warlock?"

So I'll bring you up to date.

This is something that's extremely difficult for me to
write about. When I began this chapter the first person on my
list was Frank Cockett, one of Habilitat's many but most successful stories. I have known Frank since February 3, 1971. I've
raised him like a son, loved him like a brother, and he was my
best friend. He was truly my best friend. He had been working
at Habilitat for thirteen years in a variety of positions. As a
matter of fact, he was in every possible position. He started the
construction business with its five divisions that provide constant vocational training for between thirty and forty residents.

Frank was admired, loved, and respected by all who came
in contact with him. He not only possessed the qualities to
work on the clinical side but he also had a tremendously fine
and sound business mind—and on top of all that, he was creative. Aside from Vickie, he had been with me the longest.
Frank was being groomed to take my place, in the not too dis-
tant future, when I decided to retire. He had all of the attrib-
utes that an executive director needed.

To make a long story short and because there is no nice
way to say this, Frank was brutally and senselessly murdered in
November of 1986. His death is still being investigated.

To say that Frank's death has been one of the toughest
things I've ever had to come to grips with is to say the least. All
of us—and the many thousands of people who knew Frank—
were and to some degree still are in shock. The only way I can
work through this is to keep on making Habilitat the best ever
in memory of a friend I loved deeply. Even though he died

Frank Cockett

The Frank M. Cockett, Jr. wing.

young and so tragically he had already made a real contribution for a better world.

Our newest building, which is right now in the process of being constructed, will be dedicated as the Frank M. Cockett, Jr. wing along with a plaque bust of him. I couldn't think of a more fitting tribute.

Habilitat's in terrific shape today. It can, more or less, run itself with all the trained and loyal people on staff, starting with Vickie right down to the newest one. We're also working on building up our cash reserve. We have to continue because we believe Habilitat is a real, workable alternative to jail or death. And we don't have any reason to think it might stop. One thing we've learned is we don't want anything from politicians except an occasional laugh. So we want to be ready— for anything.

As for my heart, I had more chest pains in 1985 while I was in Los Angeles being interviewed on the "Michael Jackson Show" after he had his own heart problems. I returned to Hawaii where I had an angioplasty in November, when a blockage in my artery was removed. (The same one I thought I could get rid of four years earlier with herb tea and a special diet.) I was in the hospital two days, home two days, and then returned to work. Since then I've had no problems.

Enough of this. Whatever happened to the kid who thought he was a warlock? He finished the program and, after working at Habilitat for a while, went into the Air Force. He worked there on a team that retrieved space capsules at sea. After that he went back to school, became a minister, and got married.

I don't know what happened to "Oscar." I never went down to the police station to pick up the skull, and I suppose they got rid of it.

Maria, who forgave her father in one of our first marathons for sexually abusing her, is another graduate who worked for us for a while. Then she, too, went back to school on the East Coast. Today she's a successful anthropologist in Southeast Asia.

Dave Braun gets a special thank you. Without him, I don't think Habilitat would've survived its first year. He taught me much about public relations and how to use a secretary properly. He is one of a kind. He had the tenacity to take anything you threw at him and turn it into gold. He got married, moved to San Francisco, and then to Alaska. He returned to the Bay Area when AIDS started getting a lot of attention in the media. Today he has dedicated his life to AIDS victims.

Remember *Jay Dodson*? He was the resident who started the Rose Garden Conspiracy. He left the program prematurely, got back into drugs and crime, then fortunately found his way back to Habilitat. The second time around, he was very serious about his life, and he graduated. He joined the staff and married Betsy, who had come into the program from the streets of Waikiki. They had a baby named Nicole in 1986, and both are now respected and essential staff members. Betsy work in administration, and Jay is director of marketing and development.

Kimo was not one of our success stories. We took him back into the program following that episode with a gun in Salt Lake, but he split again. He is now doing ten years for manslaughter in a drug-related incident.

Richie Rivera was another who tried the program twice — first as a staff member (drafted by me from Phoenix House when we started, you'll remember) and later as a resident. After that, Richie was Habilitat's PR guy, going with me to the Bel-Air Hotel for the Rickles-Newhart seminar. Well, one day Richie came into my office and announced he was getting married in a couple of days.

I was surprised. I didn't even know Richie had a girl-friend. He told me he had met her a week ago, and they were getting married right away.

I said, "Why don't you two live together for a while, see if you really want to do this?"

Richie said no, and the marriage didn't last very long. After that, Richie came to me and said it was time for him to leave Habilitat, time for him to make his own "bones" in main-stream society. I hugged him and wished him the best.

He called me in December 1985. He was in jail in Alaska on a cocaine beef. He said he needed a letter from me so maybe he could get out. I wrote the letter, and he got out, and it was some time before I heard from him. He called me that summer to say he was in Seattle, making a living and staying straight. I hope he does well.

Ron Barker was another who had a habit of slipping back into drugs. He was the guy who came to us from Synanon with *Wardell Gohlar* and their wives to help organize and run the advertising specialties business. Ron and Wardell and their wives left before the end of that year, returned to Detroit, and went back on drugs. Then all four returned to Habilitat to enter the program as residents.

Unfortunately, Wardell couldn't take the pressure, and he split after a month. Four months later, he was killed by a policeman in Detroit. Ron and the others finished the pro-gram. Ron worked at the Habilitat farm for a while, then in sales, and finally in fund-raising, a department he set up after the first telethon.

In 1978, Ron returned to Detroit and again went back on drugs. A couple of years later, he moved to California, where his situation got worse. Finally in 1983, he entered the program a second time, graduating and rejoining the staff. He has been head of induction the past two years.

Ron's wife stayed in Detroit, by the way, and they divorced. Ron has remarried, and he and his wife are raising the boy Ron had with his first wife (who is now fourteen) and the two daughters of his second wife, aged thirteen and nineteen.

Louis Povoromo, alias Joe Cascone, who hid out at Habilitat for nearly two years, finally got out of jail in New York, after becoming a born-again Christian. Last I heard, he was back home in Brooklyn and doing very well.

There are five "rabbis" I credit with making the most input—by giving their time, talent and energy, and above all, their friendship.

One is *Frank Natale*, who is still a very good friend. In a shitty move by his boss Mitch Rosenthal, Frank was ousted from Phoenix House after working to build that program for eleven years. As it turned out, it was probably the best thing that could've happened to Frank because he moved to Houston and founded the Natale Institute. His institute is now a successful operation conducting motivation seminars throughout the United States and Europe.

Frank still gives us the benefit of his experience whenever he visits us. He came in 1986 and said, "When you go for a lot of government funding, you begin to do things to satisfy local and national politicians rather than doing what you want to do to run a quality program. Your program is the best in the country."

Frank was interviewed by the media. I remembered how they had played up previous interviews with Frank— especially the one where Frank said I had a big mouth and needed to learn how to be a better fund-raiser. That time, an entire page was devoted to me and Habilitat. Now we were lucky to get ten inches buried on an inside page and no photo. I can call a state senator a moron and get front page coverage, but when I get an expert sitting here saying we have the best or one of the two best drug rehabilitation programs in the world, nobody's interested. How do you figure?

Well, nobody ever said life was fair.

Another top rabbi over the years has been *Frank Haines*, who joined the Habilitat board only a couple of weeks before the state audit was announced and all hell broke loose. He was a well-respected member of the community and the president of Architects Hawaii, one of the state's largest architectural firms. He didn't need that shit. But he put me under his wing and taught me what to do, how to do it, and why and when to do it.

We had trouble with insurance, and he set up meetings with the top people in the insurance industry. We had trouble with the courts, and he set meetings with the chief justice. If it wasn't for Frank after that audit, Habilitat would've been closed. Of course, if you ask him, he's humble enough to deny it. But that's not so.

Frank taught me a lot about the business of politics and how to approach the politicians, even though some of them were unapproachable, and I mean totally. He also taught me about parliamentary procedure during board meetings and how to deal with board members when we had a potential personality clash. He has a way of breaking something down so the most intelligent person and the lowest form of moron can both understand what he is saying.

Yet, what I love about him most is he's just a good person. Frank is the kind of person who doesn't want to be on a board where he can't make a contribution and cause positive change. I'm happy to say that he is still on our board.

When Frank joined Habilitat, he said he wouldn't change me, and I wasn't to try changing him. We'll we've both influenced each other a lot.

Karen White was like my second mother. She tried every-thing she could do to put a muzzle on my mouth, to follow after everything I did and apologize. When I first came to Hawaii, she was on the board of Communiversity. At the time, the program needed more residents desperately if it was to survive so I ran around all over the island, pulling people out of hospitals and jails, wherever I could get them. I didn't know it, but everybody was turned off by my approach, by my New York ways.

Because Karen worked for the family court, a lot of the people I was dealing with knew her. Before long, she got com-plaints from Koolau, Circuit Court, the Hawaii State Hospital, Oahu Prison, Halawa jail, and the detention home. So she called me and said, "Let's have lunch."

I said, "What's happening? To what do I owe the honor of this lunch?"

"Vinny, you're going about it wrong. You're not recogniz-ing the local customs and culture. People operate very slowly in Hawaii."

"Well," I said, "they got to change."

Karen said, "Yes, but slowly. There's a process you have to go through here to do what you want."

I had to go back to the heads of all those institutions and apologize. And I think that's what made us close. Karen did not expect me to do that.

Karen served on Habilitat's board for many years. When she had to resign, it was a sad occasion for both of us. "I love you, I love Habilitat," she said, "but the Ethics Commission came down with a ruling that there is the possibility of a conflict of interest with me being on the board and working with family court in my present capacity."

Karen continued to come out to the facility to rap with the kids. She knew how to listen, and she really cared. It's the

Dave Braun

Ron Barker

Karen White

Mary Ann Bigelow

greatest feeling for her to help a kid. She knew when someone was trying to con her, and she would straighten them out. She wouldn't ever come to us about it, but the kids would. Then I'd go to Karen and ask why she didn't say something. She'd say, "Vinny, it's no big thing."

Karen is one in a million. That song must've been written for her.

Without Frank Haines after 1978, we wouldn't have gotten where we are. Before that, it was *Jerry Greenspan*. I called him "Greenscrooge," and if we kidded around a lot, it was mostly all business with him. He has the keenest financial brain I ever saw. He taught me everything about financial statements and being cost effective.

He used to talk a lot about where I was going with Habilitat. He'd ask, "What do you want to do? How many facilities do you want? Aren't you better off with just one place in order to keep control?"

He was one of my most loyal board members. Although he was one of the members who put me on probation in the early days, that wasn't his idea—it was something he had to do in his position of president. Jerry lives in California today, has homes in San Francisco and San Diego, and owns a chain of lighting fixture stores.

Right from the beginning, *Dave Schutter* has been one of my top rabbis. A lot of times he didn't tell me what I wanted to hear, and often he said things I didn't like. But that's what friends are for.

I don't know how many hours of free time Dave has given us. To this day, any time I have a question that involves a criminal or civil thing, I'll call Dave. He'll tell me what I should or shouldn't do, and he won't charge me.

Other people have figured as stars in Habilitat's story so far too. You could not take a shot at me or Habilitat over the years without incurring *Aku's* wrath. Aku was controversial, but he talked straight, and he was the most successful person- ality in the history of Hawaiian radio. And he *always* supported Habilitat.

In the midst of my attack from Duke Kawasaki, the news- papers, and his callers, Aku would stop his show and say, "Vinny, wherever you are, this is for you and your troops." And then he would play "My Way."

After the record stopped, he'd say, "Keep doing what you're doing. Don't worry about Duke Kawasaki. What goes around comes around. He'll get his."

It felt good to know that Aku was a true friend. A true friend is there through thick and thin. He never once called me to ask, "Is this right? Is this wrong?" He knew I was clean and that the attack was bullshit.

I was on the mainland promoting my autobiography when he went into the hospital with a respiratory illness. They thought maybe it was pneumonia. But Aku had always been a big smoker, and they discovered lung cancer. He was operated on, then released, and he went home. When I got back to the islands, I called his daughter, and she told me he wasn't seeing anyone. He died in July of 1983. He had been replaced at KSSK (K-59 Radio) by another old friend, Larry Price, the ex- University of Hawaii football coach who had turned into an investigative reporter. He and a veteran disc jockey named Michael W. Perry took over Aku's morning show. The day after Aku died, they read a letter he had written to say goodbye to his faithful listeners:

"Folks—the news is—I didn't make it. Now hold on: I know it's a sad piece of news and I'm sorry to lay it on you this way—but for some reason I feel up about it rather than down."

The reason Aku felt positive? His listeners had heard he was sick, and thousands of letters poured in, creating what he called "the force—the force of contentment, well-being and peace that surrounds me now."

"Well—where do we go from here?" he asked. "Wouldn't it be great if there *really* were a big golf course in the sky—and folks *really* could wind up playing there. Now you listen, that's the thought I'm holding for whenever my time is up down here. And folks I wish there were some way I could make you know how much I've loved you all through the years."

Aku was sixty-six and definitely a unique human being.

Mary Ann Bigelow still lives next door, and she is as lovable or feisty as each situation calls for. When we moved into her old home, the place was hidden in a forest of trees. I have to confess not many are left. We cut most of them down to make room for new buildings.

There was one tree I told Arthur Saiki to get a chain saw and take down. He didn't look to see if Mary Ann's car was in the driveway the way we usually did. It was, and she came rushing over after hearing the saw. By then the tree was on the ground, and she was screaming for me. I snuck out and went to Hab II, where I worked for three days. I figured she'd have to calm down after three days.

But as soon as she saw my car, she came running over. I knew I was in for it so I rounded up Saiki and the others who helped him cut the tree and told them I was going to them a figazy haircut. I lined them up in front of Mary Ann and let them have it. I was yelling at the top of my lungs. It went on for half an hour. When I was finished, I told the troops I wanted them to plant that tree back in.

Mary Ann said, "Vinny, that tree took two hundred years to grow."

Mary Ann loved her trees and the foliage, but we needed space for our buildings. So many trees came down, and she really understood.

Noise has always been a problem with so many people living here. Sometimes our games got pretty loud, and because
Mary was our closest neighbor, she had to put up with the
most. When we moved in, in 1971, we promised we'd soundproof the buildings. I'm afraid it was 1983 before we had the
money to soundproof anything.

Even so, Mary Ann became a second grandmother for
me and a grandmother to Habilitat. It's a title she wears with
pride. When she first gave us an option to buy the property,
her friends and neighbors called her up and told her she was
nuts to let an insane New Yorker move in with a bunch of row-
dies. Some of them figured she had gone off the deep end, and
they all said she'd regret it. Not long ago, she told me she hasn't
regretted it once.

For a long time there was bad blood between *Gerard
DeLisio* and me. I didn't mind him leaving Habilitat, even
when I needed help so badly. I just didn't like the way he did
it, sneaking his stuff out of the facility bit by bit and never telling me goodbye — especially when I was in the hospital for
back surgery. He could've told me ahead of time that he was
leaving, and he could've stayed on until I recuperated. I
should've known, from the time when we were looking at the
Habilitat structure chart and he saw the board of directors on
top, then my name, then his. He said at the time, "I can never
be number one here."

Gerard always had a goal to get a Ph.D. in psychology.
After working at a number of jobs, he ended up running a
drug program in Hawaii for the Marines. Through the years,
he's kept up his schooling, and I'm happy to report that his
Ph.D. is getting very close. I'm also happy to say that Gerard
and I are now friends again. I still don't think what he did was
fair, but our friendship is more important.

I can't think of anything we did that had to do with

entertainment that *Ethel Azama* wasn't part of—telethons, concerts, and in-house events. The early luaus, all the fund-raisers, the high school graduations, you name it, Ethel was there with her incredible voice.

Her son Joby had brain cancer when he was a little kid, and his doctor had a son in our program so later when Joby had problems in school, the doctor suggested Ethel bring the boy to me. Joby went into the program for the summer.

Later, in January 1984, Joby came back into the program. He was nineteen then. Ethel didn't say so, but I personally think she knew she was going to die. At the time, she was hav-ing trouble with her daughter, Shay, who was fifteen. Nothing serious—her marks went down at school, she was hanging out with the wrong people. With this in mind, Ethel had set a meeting for Friday at Habilitat. Things came up, and I had to postpone it until Monday, and she died Sunday. It was my job to tell Joby.

We arranged it with the police department to get a motor-cycle escort from Kaneohe all the way to Hawaii Kai—a little difficult because we had no hearse. But they were nice about it. Again, we all wore Habilitat tee-shirts, paid our respects, and left.

Not long after she died, Ethel's ex-husband brought Shay to see me. After a lengthy conversation, it was decided that Shay would come into the program. Her father felt she would do better with Joby in Habilitat.

Joby and Shay both graduated from the program and today both come to visit their "Uncle Vinny" and "Aunt Vickie" on a regular basis. We will never forget their mom.

Dick Jensen was another entertainer who was always ready to help. For a long time, he had a thing with drugs—coke, pot, booze but predominantly coke. For years I tried to talk him out of it. Numerous times in his dressing room he'd smoke a joint and do some coke in front of me. I think he would've been a very big star if it wasn't for the drugs. He had a good run in Las Vegas for a while, and he was called the "Giant." But the handwriting was on the wall when he was singing at the Oceanic, a floating nightclub.

It all came crashing down in July 1983 (the same month Aku died), when Dick was arrested on cocaine charges. Less than a month later stories in the paper told about how Dick was a born-again Christian, and some people began to gossip. They said Dick found religion in order to beat the coke rap. But it was true, Dick *was* a believer. When he pleaded guilty to the charges against him, the court showed leniency, giving him a five-year suspended sentence and a $2,000 fine. To this day, Dick is clean, and he remains active in his church.

Now for the politicians and assorted civil servants.

Duke Kawasaki is still a state senator, and I'm happy to say that we've buried the hatchet.

At this point, in my opinion, *Dennis MeeLee* doesn't have much longer to be head of mental health. This is a gubernatorial election year, and perhaps he should look for another job.

Speaking of elections, *Cec Heftel,* who suggested we do a telethon and then provided the air time, gave up his interest in Hawaii television, and was elected to the U.S. Congress. He recently resigned his seat in the House of Representatives and ran for governor of Hawaii. He didn't win, he was beaten by the Lieutenant Governor who is now Governor, John Waihee.

When *Ray Belnap* was head of the prison system and falling asleep in meetings, I told the media he ought to be a farmer. To the best of my understanding — and to my surprise — he is now a farmer.

Frank Fasi lost his spot in the mayor's office in 1980 and regained it in 1984. He is still a friend.

Vickie Marino

Mayor Frank Fasi

Frank Marino

Finally, my family. My brother *Frank Marino* has his own sales business in New Jersey and is doing well. After running the cookie operation, our daughter *Lila* is now gainfully employed outside Habilitat and is also doing well.

Vickie is still clinical coordinator and number two in the Habilitat structure. Aside from her regular duties, she now has everybody going crazy doing aerobics. It's very hard to keep up with her.

And *Victoria* is now eleven years old—going on thirty-five.

EPILOGUE

A lot of today's kids are very insecure. They wonder about the use of getting an education and struggling for a career when the threat of nuclear war hangs overhead. Kids see that their parents have settled for what they consider mediocre lives and that they often preach the exact opposite of what, in reality, they do. These kids have a low sense of self-worth and self-esteem. Their attitudes are summarized in the slogan: "Live for today, feel good, get high, and the hell with tomorrow. It probably won't come anyway, and if it does, then get high again." Many of the kids in this country are running away from the reality they see. They don't like what they're seeing, and this contributes to the high rate of teenage suicide.

I have to lay most of the fault in the parents' laps. Parents

often model the wrong values—materialism and dishonesty—
in their daily lives, while they preach the opposite when talking to their children.

Parents, themselves, succumb to peer pressure to keep up
with the Joneses, while they preach the importance of becoming an individual and an independent thinker to their child.
Parents harp on the dangers of drugs to their children while
they smoke and drink in their presence.

While stressing frugality and planning ahead to the children, adults constantly live above their means. If deprived of a
paycheck for a month or six weeks, many would be bankrupt.

I look at Habilitat the way society looked at hospitals years
ago when they brought people to them to die—places of last
resort. I foresee that many public state-run schools will be
closed, and children will be educated in private boarding
schools that implement modified versions of Habilitat's philosophies. These schools will be run by people who are the role
models that kids no longer find at home.

So many parents fail to realize that their behavior is their
children's role model. Instead they operate on the theory of,
"Do what I say, not what I do." Children come into the world
totally uninhibited, and from that day on, their parents are
their role models. They learn values, morals, ethics, everything
from their parents or those who care for them while they're
growing up to become attorneys, physicians, astronauts,
junkies, thieves, whatever.

The private schools I envision will teach, by example, values, ethics, honesty, trust, and good working habits. They will
also maintain a system of genuine rewards for good behavior
and inevitable and unfailing discipline for bad behavior. In
addition they will emphasize proprietorship and the ability to
stand by one's convictions, based on common sense and logic.
The teaching and role modeling will stress not being caught

up by peer pressure or the need for being accepted. In essence such schools will do what Habilitat does now—teach the individual to be an individual.

Such a boarding-school concept, already represented by many private schools, will be more cost effective. It will capture the potential of students on an individual instead of a collective basis and they will create an aura of positive peer pressure that will affect many kids' lives for the better.

The main reason Habilitat needs its highly structured program is because many parents do not realize how little time the family spends together as a unit. This means little or no time is available to pass on values and talk about problems. Children don't spend enough time with their parents to learn from them.

I am sure when asked about it, most parents would say their time with their children is quality time. In most cases that's absurd. Examine how much time most parents actually spend with their children. In our present society the economic structure is such that both parents usually have to work, and where does this leave the kids?

If they're young enough, they're in the care of babysitters, nursery schools, or kindergartens during most of their waking hours. Later they attend elementary school, then intermediate or junior high and high school. After school, they attend sports events, go places with their friends, or spend time at home alone as latch-key children.

Parents come home at 5:30 or 6:00 PM, tired, often irritable, with their own chores to do and dinner to prepare. Then they think, why not have a drink to help unwind. It's certainly more enjoyable than playing with the kids or helping them with their homework. Dinner time includes a little light conversation; then after their meal, most families spend the rest of their evening watching the boob tube.

Count up the hours per week—perhaps I should say minutes per week—spent in meaningful communication. I'm not talking about arguing or bickering; I'm talking about real communication—a sharing of thoughts, ideas, feelings, plans. How much of this really takes place?

In addition to genuine contact, kids need responsible education, with verifiable facts, about what the use of drugs actually does—the results of drug addiction. The use of threats or myths that cannot be backed up is counterproductive. Teaching children about drugs must begin when they're babies.

It is crucial that parents accept the responsibility for the early training of their infants and use their position as role models to influence their children properly. As an example, when small children hear their mother answer the telephone and tell the caller that her husband is not home when they can see that he is sitting right there, they have to assume that lying is perfectly acceptable even though they've been told not to lie.

This is where the double standard begins. Then it gets reinforced when, later on, Dad brings home office supplies "borrowed" from the office, lies to a police officer about the speed he was driving while he espouses honesty and truthfulness, or comes home obviously intoxicated while he preaches moderation. Soon the kid is pretty confused, which makes her a perfect target for peer-group individuals rebelling against parental authority.

I've often wondered why, when a child is quite small and in the first years of school, parents usually attend all school events faithfully. Later on, when peer pressure is so much stronger and the child really needs their support, many parents do not attend PTA meetings, sports events, or other school-related activities. Only a small percentage of parents—and usually the same ones—are at these meetings and games.

That's where I place a lot of fault. How many parents lead by example instead of by sermon? You won't ever be perfect, but you can try to set the best example you know how to. Above all you can be honest with your children. Whenever you take a trip into a new territory, you usually need a road map for direction. It's the same with a kid trying to grow up. He needs guidance and direction from a source he can trust.

Parents need to try to be not only a mother and/or father but also a friend their children can rely on to raise them with a system based on real rewards for good behavior and fair disciplinary action when it is called for. It's true such a system requires a lot of patience, effort, energy, and work, but I believe if enough parents did this we would have a lot fewer kids winding up in serious trouble.

Racism, bigotry, intolerance—all of these stem from parental teaching. Even if you got these from your own parents, try to weed these feeling out of what you pass on to your kids.

Show me a parent who is a giver, and I'll show you a parent who is a gainer. And by giver, I mean a person who gives something and wants nothing in return other than feeling good giving it. Show me a parent who is only a taker, always looking to take something from somebody, and I'll show you a parent who is a loser.

It's a good idea to plan a family day once a week when each family member, in turn, gets to choose something the family can do together. Maybe one Sunday Dad wants to go to the softball game, so everybody goes with him. Maybe next time Junior wants to go to the zoo, so everybody goes. The following week maybe Sis takes the family with her to the skating rink or Mom wants to go to a museum. Whatever it is, everybody joins in and makes it a family outing.

Work as well as play should be shared. Mom shouldn't be the only one who cooks and cleans; Dad shouldn't always mow

the lawn or wash the car alone. Working together with a sense
of camaraderie makes the job go a lot faster.

One or twice a month there should be a family meeting
where Mom and Dad take off their authoritative hats, and the
kids can confront them in a structured or controlled manner.
Perhaps the kids feel one or both parents are inconsiderate. For
example, they take too long in the bathroom. Maybe the kids
feel Dad's attitude is lousy, or Mom's fuse is too short. Maybe
the parents have some complaints about the kids. Parents and
children can honestly communicate and resolve areas of ten-
sion to achieve a more harmonious daily life and feeling of
family unity. All in all I believe that the lack of unity within
families is a major cause of delinquency, and the merry-go-
round has got to stop somewhere.

I also feel it's vital for parents to set up a trust line with
their children so the kids will come to them with their problems and questions before they do something they might be
embarrassed about or regret later. Families should be able to
discuss any subject, whether it's a racial issue, drug use, sex,
masturbation, possible careers, or just likes and dislikes. Parents should welcome and encourage inquiries on any subject.
It's usually much more sensible for a child to make up her
mind about a problem based on what she learns from her parents rather than from something she picks up elsewhere.

If you feel insecure about guiding and advising your
children, look into some of the many good books written
about child raising and parenting. You probably won't want to
accept verbatim what is printed in a book—just read the book
and pick and choose what is logical and what makes sense to
you. Discuss your ideas with other parents, and listen to their
input.

My mother, may she rest in peace, told me a long time ago
that we don't own our children; we only borrow them and that

being a parent is a huge responsibility. I didn't always believe her then; now I know how right she was.

To sum up, what I'm talking about is working hard at being a parent—it's the most important job you'll ever have. Learn all you can about this job. Then try to do it with intelligence, love, and understanding. Teach by example the virtues of honesty, integrity, and self-discipline. Whatever you do, don't tell your child one thing and then do another yourself. This is what I believe is necessary to raise a child successfully. If more people followed these guidelines, there would be little need for places like Habilitat.

Unfortunately, whether because parents are immature, have a bad marriage, or are just too lazy to accept responsibility for themselves and their children, places like Habilitat will probably always be in demand. Sad as it is to see, parental apathy, complacency, mediocrity, or just plain lack of love and understanding keeps places like Habilitat bursting at the seams.

It seems strange to realize that our society requires extensive training before licensing an individual to operate even an automobile, but to marry and raise human beings, all you need is a few bucks to buy the license. Most public school systems in America have classes in driver's education and home economics. How many do you know of that have classes in parenting and relationships?

Schools should also have classes where kids can learn the truth about drugs. In fact, basic alcohol and drug information is already required by law in elementary and secondary schools in most states. Unfortunately, in many areas these classes don't get much attention or funding.

What happens is that the schools resist. Some come right out and say, "We don't need it—we don't have a problem in our school." And you know what kind of barnyard that statement comes from.

Others say things like, "It's too controversial—parents won't like it." Or "The curriculum is already to crowded and, besides, there's no money to hire anybody trained to teach it." Here's another cop-out—one of the worst: "We already gave them a class about drugs, and it didn't do any good."

With attitudes like this at school, the ball goes back into the parents' court. Parents have to keep pushing the schools, and usually the best way to do this is to organize. In groups, as well as alone, parents can do a lot to bring about positive change.

To make this possible, one of the things that's urgently needed is a handbook of important and useful information about drugs and alcohol, with sound and workable advice. That's going to be my next book.

This will not be an easy book for parents to read because, as you can see from my first two books, I have a reputation for saying what I think. I believe in being out front, and if people don't like what I have to say, that's fine with me. But please don't come crying to me later when your kid turns up doomed to a wasted life.

Of course, several books are already available. Major bookstores in many cities now have entire sections devoted to drugs and alcohol. Having so much choice is in some ways as confusing as having none, especially to family members—the innocent victims who understand least and yet suffer no less than the abusive personalities who cause the feelings of loss and pain.

Much of the information currently available is fragmentary. Even more is contradictory. And some is flat-out damaging. One book written for parents goes so far as to say about cocaine: "If you must do coke, do it infrequently . . . take proper care of your nose . . . make sure you can afford it . . . make sure it's the 'real thing' and not an adulterant or substitute." Why not say if you're going to play with a gun, make sure it's loaded with real bullets, not blanks?

It's time for some straight talk, definitive questions, tough answers. Previous books aren't tough or honest enough. And as the problem accelerates, most parents react with an apathetic (yet desperate) shrug or paralytic hysteria.

I've also noticed that many parents don't even want to know if a problem's there. They say things like, "Not my kid— he wouldn't dare use drugs!" Or "He only smokes pot and drinks a little beer, thank God—no hard stuff." Others cop out by saying, "How can I say no when I've got a cocktail in my hand?"

These parents are "in denial." That means they've got their heads shoved into the sand somewhere. More than half of all parents never get out of denial, and as a consequence, they can never, ever help their child. In fact, for as long as they remain in denial, they are enabling their kid's unacceptable behavior.

"Enabling," one of the essential subjects I'll cover in the next book, is parental behavior that allows—and in some cases actually encourages—continued drug abuse in the kids. And parents don't even know they're making it worse.

There are other kinds of enablers. Besides the *denier*, there is the *bargainer*. This is the parent who promises the child some material reward (a new car, a computer, a trip to Europe) if the kid will only go back to school, see a counselor, stop hanging out with the wrong kids, quit drinking or at the very least cut down on the amount.

Another *enabler* is the *caretaker*. These are parents who believe they're totally responsible for the child—the child's abusive behavior, the consequences of that behavior, and the child's eventual cure. If the child gets into trouble at school, these parents have a ready excuse for the teachers and school administrators. If the child gets into trouble with the police, caretaker parents will bail him or her out, pat the kid on the back, say, "Maybe now you've learned your lesson," then go hire the best lawyer in town.

Caretakers try a thousand things, but nothing works. They spend weeks, months, years trying to talk sense into the kids. They plan more family outings, sign the child up for an after-school sport, take the child to church or to a round of counselors, and ricochet from one parenting philosophy to another without giving any of them a chance to work. These are parents who can think and talk of nothing else. They are obsessed. They are as addicted to their abusive child as the child is addicted to drugs.

There are other traps that parents fall into. The *good news* is that there are also ways to get out of these traps. And once out, there are things the parent can do. Let me rephrase: there are things a parent *must* do. Because if *you* don't, who will?

The parent can learn about the drugs themselves and why the kids get into them. There are about a dozen really good reasons, and you have to understand them in order to do anything about them. The parent can also learn how to confront their kids, talk to them, listen to them, and build mutual respect and trust with them.

In sixteen years, thousands of young people have come to Habilitat so we've had to learn effective ways to communicate. We've developed techniques for creating a positive self-concept. Self-esteem is the real common denominator when it comes to drugs. I've never met anyone anywhere who abused drugs or alcohol who had a high level of self-esteem.

We've learned how to teach coping and other social skills. We had to do this because a kid who blots out pain, boredom, frustration, and other emotions never learns to experience and handle these feelings. Many youthful drug abusers have also failed to develop normal conversational and participation skills. In other words, they're antisocial.

Finally, we've learned to teach a kid how to make her or his own decisions. By learning how to think independently rather than go along like a bunch of sheep, kids can say no to their peers.

Sometimes kids need a place like Habilitat, a place outside the home, and parents need to know about the various programs that are available. Parents should know a program works, and they should know what is needed to keep such programs alive.

President Reagan has made a big deal of his "war on drugs." Naturally I'm happy that he is giving drugs so much of his attention. However, I think that he and the government in general are going about a lot of what they're doing in the wrong way.

Instead of spending money on beefing up the police and border patrol and building bigger jails, they should devote their energies to drying up the demand. America is awash with drugs because there's a demand for them. If you arrest one dealer, twenty more will take his place. The answer isn't tougher laws and more police; it's more education and prevention.

What we need is money for the schools and parent groups. We also need to keep the government off the private programs' backs. Successful programs reduce the demand by removing customers from the drug market *permanently*. These programs should be nurtured—not attacked as they have been.

I'm not talking about Habilitat by the way. We are no longer funded by state or federal governments. Most other programs are. And they are getting the same sort of crap that we got for many years—a nice government grant followed by some moron with a clipboard and a thousand stupid rules.

If Ronald Reagan is going to succeed in this drug war, the funded programs should be accountable for two things only. The first is financial. There should be a yearly audit to see that the money goes where it's supposed to go. Hopefully these audits will be done by private firms that are top heavy in proprietorship rather than by government agencies noted for their mediocrity and stupidity.

The second thing drug programs should be accountable for is their success. They must set annual goals and meet them. They should bring a certain number of new residents in, move a certain number from one phase of treatment to the next, and graduate a certain number to successful independent living.

Then if their books are not clean and the programs don't work, close them down. Otherwise leave them alone.

A recent story in a very popular magazine started with these words: "An epidemic is abroad in America, as pervasive and as dangerous in its way as the plagues of medieval times. Its source is the large and growing traffic in illegal drugs, a whole pharmacopoeia of poisons hiding behind street names as innocent as grass, snow, speed, horse, and angel dust. It has taken lives, wrecked careers, broken homes, invaded schools, incited crimes, tainted businesses, toppled heroes, corrupted policemen and politicians, bled billions from the economy and in some measure infected every corner of our public and private lives."

That's not a pretty picture. It's obvious that the challenge has never been greater, but we need not feel powerless. There are things we can do.

The title of my next book will be *Everything Parents Need to Know About Drugs . . . And Are Too Terrified to Ask.*